# THE TRUTH BEHIND THE
## Smiles

**Suppression**, the silent killer.
How to find **hope**, never give up,
and cultivate **resiliency**.

Mélissa-Sue Methven

# THE TRUTH BEHIND THE *Smiles*

To request permissions, contact the publisher at
publish@joapublishing.com

Front Cover Photo by Click Photography
Back Cover Photo by Kimmie Carter with Fotome Studios

Hardcover ISBN: 978-1-961098-58-9
Paperback ISBN: 978-1-961098-57-2
eBook ISBN: 978-1-961098-59-6

Printed in the USA.

Joan of Arc Publishing
Meridian, ID 83646
www.joapublishing.com

*I dedicate this book to my children, Sophia and Matéas, who have been my most profound inspiration. They are God's gift to me and they fill my heart with joy.*

*In loving memory of my husband, Scott Allen Methven, who left us too soon but will never be forgotten.*

*We love you*

# Table of Contents

# Acknowledgments

Grateful acknowledgement is expressed to my mother— you've consistently believed in me, supported me, and guided me with unconditional love and light. You've dedicated yourself to supporting me and the kids when we've needed you the most. Thank you for moving from Osoyoos, BC, Canada to live with us after Scott's passing. And for caring for my children while I went on my five-day writing adventure, then during the countless hours I've worked tirelessly throughout the writing process. My mother is my biggest fan and I could have not accomplished writing this book without her helpfulness.

To my children, Sophia and Matéas, for your love and being my "why" for this book, thank you for seeing the importance of this message and allowing me to find the space to write.

Keira Brinton, my writing coach and publisher, thank you for turning the key that unlocked a new world for me. You believed in me and my message from the first time that I met you. I will forever cherish the most magical writing adventure with Keira in Mill Valley, California.

Francine Laliberte Launier, my editor who expertly and wholeheartedly felt the soul of my book, you are a true angel meant to edit this book.

Mindy Peterman, who did my final edit and helped me reach my timeline goal. She was such a joy to work with and she provided words of encouragement.

Furthermore, a large number of friends and family provided confidence, guidance, and support. Your encouragement is what kept my fire alive and provided me courage to write this book. Your constant messages and prayers gave me strength.

Most especially, I am grateful to the spiritual force within us all.

# Preface

I write this book with love and gratitude for you, the reader. If you are reading this, you most likely have felt a similar darkness, similar pain. If that is you, we share the same struggles. If you are here to understand how to live away from the shadows that cover the light, it is my hope and intention that my true and authentic story will help you see your truth in a way that at one time I was unable and unwilling do with my own truth. Darkness is part of our human experience and learning the tools early on for how to overcome it can save a life. My desire is that as you read this book, those seeds of faith will be planted in you, so that one day when you feel alone and isolated, you will have hope. Our experience with the dark is a crucial step in our spiritual expansion and learning period on earth.

Everything that I am sharing with you is my own personal observations and thoughts—what I hold as truth. If something within these pages does not resonate with you, I invite you to simply let it go and keep reading. I am writing this book as a friend sharing her own experience. Thank you for being the listener. I hope this helps you and is resourceful to you.

My path to writing this story was at times unguided and confusing and at other moments driven by divine interventions. That calling, the divine intervention, led me to a house among the treetops in Mill Valley, California, inspired to share my story of suppression, the loss of my husband by suicide, the struggle of raising my kids by myself after his death, my journey in the dental profession and how, even during the darkest times, I was able to find joy.

Getting to this tree house, which seemed to be floating over the beautiful lush forest, required walking down a steep staircase. Inside the house were floor-to- ceiling windows overlooking the stunning view: the scenery covered with lavish trees and a wall-to-wall blue sky. The decor of this house was purely divine with natural elements, crystals, feathers, plush fur carpets—every room perfectly decorated. This home felt sacred, a perfect environment in which to write my book. It was beautiful, comfortable, and had a serene view. I felt completely protected by all the nature surrounding me. I had three ladybugs in my room while I wrote in the early mornings.

Throughout this book I will refer to all things concerning the Divine as God, but you may call it whatever you are comfortable with. This is not a religious book by any means. I want you to feel safe here and at the same time, I want to honor what feels true to me. I do believe we are all talking about the same thing. Whether it is God, Source, Universe, or Love, we can feel His energy pulling us in guided directions and, if we truly listen to those directions, doors will open.

This is exactly what happened to me: being pulled into writing this book while also being directed to new paths and encounters with new and influential people. With each new path that opened, I could feel divine energy flowing through me. So I committed to writing this book even as I feared judgment, shame, guilt, and that darkness would come and destroy my family. I will not turn away from what I know. My faith is stronger than my fears and I trust that God will protect us.

I have this dream that my children will use this book as their guide to help them prevail over the darkness and to know that they can get out of any situation where they feel stuck. I wish this for you too. My desire is that this book reaches the one *and* the masses. I hope this book will meet you in the corners where you feel the most vulnerable, and I want you to be met with love—the love that I feel for all humans, especially those who are struggling in darkness.

My invitation is for you to lean on God or the universe or any other belief you have and pray for guidance. Allow yourself to fully trust and persevere through the resistance. **You can't escape the darkness, so you must learn to live with it and conquer it.**

If at times I seem to be repeating myself, it is just because these same events carry importance in the different parts of the book.

I know that God has walked with me because I have witnessed too many miracles along my journey to ever doubt Him.

The strong intuition that has nudged me forward has made it clear that God exists and knows me.

I send you my love and light as you embark with me on this journey as I share my story with you.

Love,

*Mélissa*

# SECTION 1

# THE
# STORY

# Chapter 1

# My Truth

I have lived a life of suppression.
It has always been there. Suppression showed up in my childhood, my marriage, motherhood, and friendships. Once I became aware of this suppression, everywhere I looked, it was there, like a persistent shadow that colored my days. It manifested as a cyst in my breast, a cyst on my vocal cord, severe acid reflux, fatigue, hair loss, loneliness, anxiety, and anger.

I felt stuck. I was stuck.

So much of my life I was taught to not speak my truth. I was told to smile, hide the pain, and be quiet.

But no more.

I speak now.

This book is my truth.

I now speak my truth so my kids can speak their own truth, so they know that living a lie will be a disservice to their souls. I want them to live a life of expression. This comes from my heart and I wish to inspire others to live through their own truth without fear of judgment or doubt. I want you to understand that you are not alone.

As you read, you will become aware that there are a lot of people living in their lies. Actually, most are.

Many are hiding their truths behind their smiles.

As you begin to speak your truth, your freedom will liberate others. We can encourage each other to see clearly, to get out of the illusion, and the only way to do that is to speak our own truth. Suppression will destroy you from the inside out. It is a worldwide disease that runs through our generations, our friends, and our neighborhoods.

In my effort to clear out suppression, I am taking the first step forward to tell my whole truth without fear.

Suppression can make you feel stuck. The fears are deep and the worry that you will never get out is heavy, but there is a way out for all of us. It will not be easy, but the hard work will give you the freedom you so desire.

You will become free. Free from the heaviness of suppression. Free from loneliness, doubt, rage, and shame. You will find peace. You will find joy. You will experience light even after the darkest storms.

I am here to tell you that even with the loss of my husband, Scott, who died by suicide, the loss we felt in a tragic lawsuit, and the aftermath of these horrific events, we—my children and I—still found joy. Happiness can still be discovered and expression after suppression will lead you to full freedom.

Chapter 2

# Let Me Tell You About Scott . . .

It felt easy, the first time I met Scott. I had been staying on a houseboat in the Okanagan Valley, British Columbia. He arrived in the morning, handsome, charismatic, and quick with a smile. He was 6'4, had green eyes, light brown hair, and broad shoulders.

There was a large group on the houseboat, but the two of us enjoyed sitting and talking all day at the front of the boat. We learned we had a mutual love for music and the outdoors. He was dreaming of opening his own dental practice. We definitely felt attraction for one another. Everything at the beginning was exciting. It was easy. We had the same friends. We had the same interests. We had chemistry.

After that day, Scott and I remained friends for several years. It was easy to stay in contact because we had mutual friends and moved in similar circles. He would visit his best friends often in BC, where I lived. Scott had moved from Michigan to Alaska after dental school to pursue his dental career. After a few years of being an associate he saw an opportunity to open a practice in Wasilla, Alaska. During those years, I was also working as a private-jet flight attendant.

In June 2005, my schedule took me to Alaska for a week and Scott was the person I called. We made plans and before I knew it he was picking me up at four o'clock that sunny morning in Alaska, the land of 24-hour sun in the summers. We fished all day on a semiprivate charter boat. We knew there was chemistry and so did the others onboard. "Are you sure you aren't more than friends?" asked a friendly person on the boat. From that trip on, things moved very quickly. Because I was a flight attendant, I was able to commute easily to Alaska. After several years of commuting for work to Vancouver, BC, I decided to pursue a dental hygiene career.

Scott was a big guy and sometimes I felt like there was a little boy stuck inside his massive body. While I don't have all the answers to what Scott felt, I know he was disconnected from parts of himself that never felt loved: that smaller, lonelier part of him that, like any young boy, just *wanted* to be loved. He showed that part of himself through his generosity and had a beautiful way of loving others, but that did not fill the void he felt daily.

He avoided the pain he felt inside himself and that ultimately led to his death. His motto was, "Keep numbing and keep going." You will never know Scott personally, but through these stories I want you to know who he was so that you might recognize something of yourself or a loved one.

This is my story, and Scott's life, and death, are a large part of it. Above all else, Scott was just doing what he was taught. As a young boy he was never taught how to manage his emotions. He only knew what he had learned. He was the most generous man and everyone was his friend. He was strong, and he was appreciated by all the people he came into contact with. He was playful and bright and he shared a joke easily. He had a way of making me laugh. His dream of having a big family was fulfilled. He loved our family and he loved me.

Scott's passing created a ripple effect that was felt by thousands of people.

One magnificent life left this earth and he will never be forgotten.

# Chapter 3

# The Smiles that Hide the Truth

When we worked together we had a blast. Lingering stares and flirtatious exchanges in front of coworkers gave the veneer of love. My laughter at his quick wit was the balm to the pain I felt. Scott had a great sense of humor and he knew how to make everyone laugh with his sarcasm and he seemed to have memorized all kinds of jokes. He liked it when I worked at the office. No one suspected that the roles of "loving husband and wife" we consistently acted out at work were the lie to the reality of our relationship at home.

When gathering with friends, I could escape from the reality of our relationship. I would slap on my rehearsed smile, and together, he and I would plan the most exciting adventures. I hid the pain that was bubbling up within me under my smile.

I did not want to ruin the fun energy with my negative marital stories. Instead, I suppressed them and shoved them down.

I was so good at my role that I taught my kids how to pretend too. We all smiled and continued on because that's all we knew. Truthfully, not every day was bad. The good days were sporadic, and they were distractors from the pain we were all in. Each time a good day appeared, we would hold onto it, clasping it tightly within our hands, hoping that it would never leave. Those days were built with sand that slipped through our fingers more quickly the harder we gripped, leaving the dust of what might have been hopeful.

Lately, as I have revisited our pictures and videos, the feelings from those moments have come flooding back and the enormity of the situation we were in at that time has become crystal clear. I now see past the masks of the pain.

The days of pretending are gone. No more veils. No more pretty, straight, white teeth to distract from the pain pushed deep down to where no one can see and where no one will notice. Only the truth is left to stand in the aftermath of the earthquake that shook our lives. The house of dreams that Scott and I had built—of raising our family and growing old together—was destroyed in that upheaval. The rubble left behind are memories and jagged pieces of the past. After I cleaned up all of the scattered parts of the life we had built together, I stood in the middle of it all and realized the truth is all I had left.

My story contains the beauty and the beast. I will not hold back either of these parts of my truth. I am sharing it with you in hopes that you may find healing within these pages. There is always light within the dark.

I'll always hold dear the beautiful times, especially the good days when Scott would make us laugh with his incredible sense of humor. He had a talent for jokes, especially with our kids, Sophia and Matéas. The kids often ask me to share jokes like their dad used to, but I'm not great at it and usually end up googling some of them. My kids are the ones now telling jokes to me and it's something that reminds us dearly of Scott.

During my girls' weekends, checking in with Scott meant receiving ridiculously funny text messages from him that would make all of us girls burst out laughing. He had a knack for bringing joy into our lives.

We cherished fishing with Scott because that was when he was at his happiest. In those moments, he seemed at peace, genuinely immersed in his passion. I loved the calmness he exuded, especially when I caught a fish. He was so proud of me and beamed with joy.

Scott would often play his guitar at home and he was very talented at it. We would sit in the living room and sing and dance along with him. We shared the same passion for music and planned many music festival getaways. When we were at these festivals it was like we were returning to when we first met. We laughed, danced, sang, and met so many new friends. We both loved meeting new like-minded people. Scott was very social and could talk about any subject. He was charismatic and very smart about almost every topic. These fun memories carried me through the hard times. This is the Scott I knew him to be in his truth. Scott was kind, generous, smart, and funny. I felt safe with him. He gave the best hugs and the warmest smile. Because he was so tall, I could find him anywhere in any room and I knew he could keep an eye on me if I ever needed him.

One cherished memory is when Scott bought these cool science experiments to do with Matéas, knowing how much Matéas loved them. Watching Scott engage in these activities with the kids, especially our son, expanded my love for him. It felt like the ideal family dynamic I yearned for. Scott's enthusiasm for fishing also left a lasting impact on Matéas, who now shares the same passion.

Scott and I enjoyed creating backyard fires, listening to music, and watching the kids play outside. These souvenirs hold a special place in our hearts, especially on challenging days.

Our greenhouse, where Scott taught me about gardening, was another shared love. We both had a passion for a life filled with eggs from our chickens and homegrown vegetables and fruits. Raising our kids surrounded by nature was something we both cherished. Knowing my love for the beach and sunshine, Scott planned multiple beach vacations for our family

Not every day was bad. There were beautiful moments held within the container of pain. I love Scott deeply. The beauty and the pain are held together by the love we shared.

# Chapter 4

# Snorkels and Sunshine

**M**onday, **March 7, 2022** was the day it all started to fall apart. At that time, we were staying at our condo in Maui to be with Scott's father, who was nearing the end of his battle with lung cancer. We had gathered as a family to spend his last days together with him. However, after only a week, his father decided he wanted to spend his final days in his home in Dundee, Oregon. He missed his dog, Boo, and wanted to be by his side one last time. As a family, we all made arrangements to make this wish come true. I rented an extra oxygen tank for his flight from Maui to Oregon. We called the fire department to help us transport my father-in-law from the second story condo to the car. Family members booked flights with Scott's dad to Oregon. But we did not. Scott did not want to go. I felt we needed to go and I wanted to be on that flight with them to be of assistance and support. I couldn't understand at that moment why Scott didn't want to go. Then it dawned on me that this was too hard for him. It was too much for him to see his father in his last days. When it came time for Scott's father to leave Maui, Scott had to painfully say goodbye for the last time. We knew when we sent his father home on the airplane, it would be our final time with him. His cancer had spread and the doctor had let us know that he only had a few days left to live.

As fate would have it, that exact day is also when Scott found out he had lost the lawsuit that had been a seven-year battle. That battle had taken the very life out of Scott. The fight he fought every day for seven years ended in tragic loss.

## Tuesday, March 8 through Wednesday, March 9, 2022

This particular morning felt different. Scott woke up with unusual energy and excitement. He told me that he had made a spontaneous decision to plan a visit with our friends in Lanai, Hawaii. He swiftly booked our ferry tickets for the next day. Sophia and Matéas were thrilled to sense this positive shift in his energy, and they were especially looking forward to seeing their best friends, who were also our neighbors back home in Alaska and with whom they attended school. Naturally, it was a treat for them to spend the day together at the beach.

Our friends suggested a beach day with snorkeling on Hulopo'e beach for our visit. The next day, Wednesday, March 9th, filled with anticipation, we woke up early and drove to the ferry in Lahaina near the Banyan tree. After boarding the ferry, we gathered outside at the stern of the boat, ready for the day's adventure.

We all stopped to look out at the beauty of Hawaii and the wake of the waves. We saw whales and dolphins jumping out of the water. Hawaii's beauty brought joy and calmness into our hearts. Hawaii has always been a great place of healing for us. We soon arrived at the Lanai port and saw our friends waiting for us with big smiles and welcoming hearts. It was the true Ohana feeling.

Our friends drove us to the Hulopo'e Bay beach where they had set up hammocks and chairs for our day together. I remember looking at Scott and thanking him for wanting to take us there because I knew he was not a fan of the beach. He had never enjoyed sitting in the sun. He looked at me with his beautiful smile and said that he was enjoying himself too.

As I heard Scott talking with our friends, his tone and energy gave me hope. It was like I was seeing the Scott I remembered. For over a year, I hadn't recognized my husband; he had become a completely different person—almost a stranger—from the one I had married. At that moment, I thought that he could finally see the love that surrounded him and that we, as a family, would be all right. I really believed that since the lawsuit had ended, he would now be able to do more things that he loved. Hope entered my heart as we relaxed into our beach chairs.

I saw happiness in his eyes and that gave me reassurance. We decided to go snorkeling. Scott opted to wear his goggles without the snorkel tube. He could hold his breath for long periods of time and was an excellent swimmer. He would dive down to the bottom of the ocean and bring back up sand or he would go and point out sea life for the kids to see. We spent time admiring the most beautiful varieties of fish: parrotfish, trumpet fish, lemon butterflyfish, yellow tang, Moorish idol, and many more. All of us were in absolute awe of the beauty that lived in the ocean.

After swimming and playing in the water for hours, we returned to the beach and our friends cooked us a wonderful BBQ. Sophia and Matéas played with their friends and laughed loudly. As we walked to the tide pools, Scott and I held hands. We had not held hands like this for a long time. It felt so good. We explored the bay and saw hermit crabs, sea cucumbers, and sea stars. Joy filled my heart. I could feel Scott becoming himself again and so much relief poured over me.

At the end of that wonderful day, as a family we packed up our gear and got on the 5 p.m. ferry ride back to Lahaina on Maui. We waved goodbye to our friends from the top of the ferry. Everyone was smiling and happy for the blessed day that we had. Scott looked at me and said that he wanted to start reading marriage therapy books together. He suggested that when we got back home to Alaska that we could read a chapter a day. Scott had always refused to go to counseling so he had bought many books on strengthening marriages. I felt hope arising within me again. Even though I knew that we needed more than just books, this was a hopeful start to our much-needed healing. I knew that he would need to go to a recovery center for addiction before our marriage could really heal, but I was grateful for his willingness to begin something with me.

Back at our condo that evening, I prepared a steak dinner for us. The memories of this beautiful day were still fresh in our minds. Scott seemed to also feel content as we all sat around the dinner table and ate . . . until he picked up his phone and read numerous emails regarding the loss of the lawsuit. He realized in that moment that there was no more hope for our perceived truth to ever emerge. It was finalized.

Instantly, his demeanor shifted and the darkness returned. While the kids and I slept that night, Scott remained awake. I heard him getting up frequently, while I ebbed in and out of sleep all night. My attention focused on him, I wondered about his activities in our one bedroom space that held two queen-sized beds.

I remember that at one point, he asked me for the keys to the closet where we kept our personal items whenever we left and rented the condo to other travelers. I found it odd, since it was already unlocked and it seemed unnecessary to bother me with that request at 1 a.m. I told him the keys were in my suitcase and then I went back to sleep. I don't think Scott slept much that night.

The next morning, he was on his phone again and a heavy darkness seemed to surround him. I recognized this darkness; it was visible in his eyes. I assumed it was frustration and anger about losing the case and the financial settlement involved with the loss. That's all I thought this darkness represented—anger toward the legal situation. Scott mentioned he would be attending a private jiujitsu session with his favorite professor in Lahaina. Knowing his passion for jiujitsu, and being a supportive wife, I encouraged him, as usual. He enjoyed studying this martial art and watching the ultimate fighting championship with his friends.

I told him I'd take the kids to the beach until he got back.

# Trigger Warning

**Attention Readers:**

The following chapter contains material that some readers may find distressing or triggering. Topics addressed in this chapter include:

- **Suicide, death**

Please proceed with caution and take care of your mental and emotional well-being. If you feel uncomfortable or need support, consider skipping this chapter or seeking help from a trusted individual or mental health professional.

# Chapter 5

# The Goodbye I Never Imagined

**Thursday, March 10, 2022**

It was morning and my kids and I had a full day of beach time ahead of us. I packed our beach bag and lathered my six-year-old son and eight-year-old daughter with sunscreen, their pale skin made paler by the smears and streaks I so carefully rubbed into their small bodies. We said our ritual good-bye to Scott: "We love you!" We also told him to enjoy a nap and his jiujitsu lesson later on in the day. We walked out of our condo and headed down the stairs for the five-minute walk to Kaanapali Beach, a walk we had taken hundreds of times before. I sat down on a beach towel and relaxed while I watched my kids run into the ocean for a swim. They loved swimming in the water and always dove right into the waves. I smiled as I listened to their laughter and embraced their joy. They took a break from swimming and came to sit by me to build a sandcastle with a moat. Seeing them play together filled my heart with love. Everything was so beautiful and perfect.

Suddenly, out of nowhere, I was hit with a tsunami wave of sadness flowing to my heart. I knew that this sadness was coming from my husband. I could feel the pain he was in right then. This week had been so heavy. Just three days earlier he'd had to say his last goodbye to his father and lost the lawsuit. With this sadness filling my heart and the heaviness covering my body, I quickly grabbed my phone and texted Scott a short message: *I want to thank you for the beautiful day we had yesterday and I want you to know that we love you very much.*

He replied, *Don't come up and send security.*

I panicked as I read his words and rapidly replied, *Scott don't hurt yourself, we love you and I am coming up right now with the kids.* I thought if I said that I was coming up with the kids he would not do anything to harm himself.

This was the very first time he had ever called out for help. He had never talked about experiencing suicidal ideation. I had asked him many times before and he always reassured me that he did not struggle with suicidal thoughts. Instead, he always replied, "I am not depressed. I am just sad that my father is dying and the lawsuit is so hard." He always insisted that he would be okay and most importantly, that he was in control.

I told my kids that we needed to leave right away because Dad was sad and we needed to go help him. To my surprise, without any hesitation, the kids came running and we hurried up the stairs to our condo. I hadn't called security because I knew how long it could take them to actually come and help. I knew that I would be much faster than any security guard and my gut had told me to run fast.

I grabbed my key and looked my kids directly in their eyes and told them to stay in the hallway. I took a deep breath and asked God to protect me for what I might see once I opened the door.

I opened the door and turned left toward the bedroom and it was then that I saw my husband. At that moment my life changed. My heart seemed to stop, I felt a tightening in my throat, and I was in disbelief of what I was seeing. I had hoped that I had made it in time and that we might be able to save Scott.

I quickly ran back out to my children and called 911. My hands were shaking. My kids were feeling my fear and stress and they were wondering what had happened to their father. Somehow I was still able to speak and quickly blurted out that he had *gotten hurt*.

I didn't want my kids to hear what had actually happened, so I walked down the hallway and quietly talked to the 911 operator. While telling the operator everything I had seen, I realized that I wanted to go back in and start doing CPR. I told the operator that I was going back to the room. The operator said okay to this but told me to keep her on the line. I told my kids again to wait outside and that I was going to go help Dad. They agreed and I went back into our condo.

I untied Scott and started performing CPR. It had only been maybe six to nine minutes since his text to me. I felt there could be a chance to save him. I could never live with myself if I didn't try.

I remember fumbling with my hands trying to untie him. The knot was so tight and I barely had any strength left in my body to untie it but finally, I was able to release him and I laid him down on the floor. I felt for a pulse and could not find one.

So, I immediately started CPR until the paramedics arrived. I was shocked and grateful at how fast they showed up. The second they took over with CPR I ran to my kids. I gave them big hugs. We were all bawling and shaking.

All of a sudden, I felt the need to run away from there. My heart was guiding me to take my children away. I knew that they did not need to see their father being rolled out on a stretcher in the state he was in. I grabbed their hands and we walked quickly to the beach hut where I knew one of the condo's staff members. After years of us returning to vacation there, he had become like family to us. He was all I had. All of our family had flown back to Oregon to be with Scott's father during his last days of battling cancer.

I quietly told the staff member what just happened and asked him if he could stay with the kids so I could talk to the paramedics, and to police if they were to call me. He lovingly said yes and stayed with us as we sat on the grass near the beach hut. We sat for what felt like days, waiting for any news.

I called my mother-in-law to share the most horrific message I have ever had to share. She was next to her husband, Scott's father, who had only days to live. I could hear her shock and heartbreak. This was the most crippling news, and I would have to tell everyone. I remember feeling as though this was all a bad dream, but then I saw two police officers coming our direction. At first I felt relieved and thought they would give me good news about how Scott was doing. I still had hope that we were going to be able to save him.

However, instead they told me that they could not leave my side because this case was under investigation. I would have to be interviewed by a detective.

I was in disbelief. I had just witnessed the most horrific scene of my life and within minutes I was being *investigated*?! They asked if I had gotten into a fight with my husband. I told them no. I gave them my phone to show them the text messages we had exchanged just prior to the event. Nothing made sense. My whole world had just been turned upside down. I was in shock and shaking heavily.

I sat down and waited with my kids. More staff from the condo came to help and to simply sit with us. They talked with my kids and were great at helping console them. I looked around at the vacationers and sensed that everyone was wondering what was happening. I could feel them trying to understand why I had two tall policemen standing beside me. It was an uncomfortable feeling to deal with on top of what I had just encountered in our condo.

Finally, after maybe 30–40 minutes, someone came over and told me that I needed to come to the lobby. They had some questions for me. I left my kids with the staff and a friend and I walked toward the lobby. There, I saw my husband on the stretcher and asked why he was not already at the hospital. The paramedics told me that he was breathing and that they were taking him to the hospital for more tests. I was so relieved and thought that I had saved him. This would be the beginning of his recovery. He would finally accept help and we would stand by him every step of the way.

The paramedics asked me if I wanted to come to the hospital. Kids under age 12 were not allowed in the trauma department, so I answered no, because I knew my kids needed me right then. I did not want to be away from them for that long. It was almost an hour drive to the hospital and I knew my kids were scared, confused, and sad. They needed their mom. The paramedics let me know that they would call me once they received all the test results. In a daze, I said okay and watched as they took Scott away in the ambulance.

After they left I noticed everyone staring at me. Looking around, I noticed a dear friend who lived in Maui was standing in the lobby. She walked directly to me and gave me a big hug. I felt wrapped in her comfort and finally felt peace for a moment.

When I got back to Sophia and Matéas, I told them that I was hopeful that everything was going to be okay. There were more phone calls to make and I did my best to remember all the people I needed to reach. My mind was not functioning right and it was like my memory had left. All of a sudden, I remembered a few friends, Carol and Barry, who lived in Maui during the winter months. These friends were like family to us, and so I called them for help. I was not alone anymore and my kids had people that could take care of them. Carol and Barry took Sophia and Matéas to their condo with them.

I was then told that it was time to meet with the detective. Because I didn't have anything to hide, I answered every question without feeling nervous. After an hour of questioning, the detective let me know that it was no longer an investigation, and relief filled my body.

It was around 6 p.m. when someone from the hospital called and told me that I needed to come to the hospital right away. I quickly told our friends where I needed to go and that I would drive myself. My friend Shirley said, "No, you can't do that, I will drive you." I was okay but obviously my friends could tell that I was in shock and in no condition to drive. I didn't like burdening people and asking for help, but finally I agreed to let her drive me.

The experience at the hospital was very much run like it had been during Covid. Everyone was required to wear masks and only a few people could come in at a time. I remembered feeling suffocated because I was hyperventilating and crying while wearing the mask.

We walked into the trauma center and a doctor greeted us in the lobby. He sat down beside me and told me the tests showed that my husband was 100% brain-dead. There was no other function working except his breathing, since that is the last thing that goes when a person dies. They were keeping him alive with machines but the chances of recovery would only be through machine assistance.

I was permitted to go into Scott's room. I stood up to walk through the main doors of the trauma center and Shirley followed me. As we walked through the hallway we saw other patients hooked up to machines, fighting for their lives in their rooms. When we finally reached Scott's room, I walked in and was extremely shocked to see him hooked up to all of this medical equipment. I embraced him and laid my head on him. I told him that I loved him, was so sorry that he was in such pain, and that I forgave him. I also asked him to protect and guide our children because they would not understand why he left us. They will forever be in pain from losing their dad.

The hospital asked me if I wanted to get someone to come pray with us. I said yes. The chaplain came into the room and placed herself across from me on the other side of the bed. As she started to pray for Scott, I placed one hand on his head and one on his heart. As we prayed, we noticed a tear stream down his cheek. We looked at each other in amazement. Because of my beliefs, I knew Scott's soul was listening and in this room. That reaffirmed to me that even though doctors said that he no longer had any of his senses, he could still hear me. I felt that he finally saw Jesus Christ and believed. I know in my heart that this is true. This remains one of my most tender and treasured moments with Scott.

It was getting late and I felt anxious to return to be with my kids. Once I was back at the hotel where we owned our condo, the manager gave me keys to my in-laws' condo, which was vacant. I went to pick up Sophia and Matéas and we walked to the condo. I felt grateful for our family friends who had taken care of my kids when I had to leave for hours. They took them for ice cream, played games with them, and created a loving atmosphere for them.

That evening, my kids were in shock and had many questions. I told them that it was not looking very good for their dad. My heart sank and I had no words that could remove their pain. I could only hold them in my arms. We all lay in bed together, talking until midnight. Nobody could sleep. My kids asked if we could watch a movie. I said yes and we watched the most colorful movie, *Rio*. We loved this movie and it was a great distraction during such a hard time. The movie finished at 2 a.m. and I told my kids that we needed to get some rest because we were all exhausted.

They both fell asleep in my arms. Not being able to sleep, I sobbed quietly and held my babies next to my heart. As I watched them sleep, it seemed as if Sophia was raised by an unseen force. She stood and made a sound like she was taking a deep breath in, then raised her arms wide and high. I watched in silence, motionless, and I knew in my soul that Scott had come for a hug. Her hands were shaking and then she gently lay back down in my arms. Soon after, Matéas sat up and held his hands up like he was receiving a hug too. Once again, I did not move and just watched in amazement. I already believed in God, angels, souls being reincarnated, but seeing this all with my own eyes reaffirmed my beliefs. I knew Scott was with us.

## Friday, March 11, 2022

Once the sun rose, my children woke up and I felt like I was floating in a nightmare. Nobody was hungry. I asked both kids if they remembered anything from the previous night but neither did. We looked out on the balcony and saw the beauty of the ocean and heard the sounds of the waves crashing on the shore. The birds were singing and we could smell the fragrances of the flowers. We didn't want to leave the room but I had to return and grab our personal items from our condo, where my husband had committed suicide.

I didn't want to leave them but there were no other options. Sophia looked at me with conviction. "I have to go with you." Without saying it directly, she was eager to return to the crime scene. She had been asking what happened to her dad and was convinced there was blood and possibly something broken. I had not allowed the kids into the condo and she thought someone else had hurt her dad. I could see that this was very important for her. I agreed, knowing that she needed to trust and believe what I had told her: *no blood, nothing broken.*

Walking to the condo, I feared that maybe there would be something that would scare her. I was doubting my decision. Maybe I should have checked first.

I unlocked the door, and we walked in. I saw the kitchen, then I turned around the corner and looked into the bathroom area where it had happened. I was relieved that there were no signs. Sophia was relieved that I had been telling the truth.

She walked into the bedroom and saw her dad's suitcase, his clothes, where he slept. She grabbed his pillow and smelled it. She could smell him and asked if she could keep his pillow. I said, "of course." She then grabbed one of his black t-shirts and put it on. It was surreal. We were in shock and disbelief that he was gone so abruptly.

I then had to go back to the hospital and talk to the doctors. My mom had flown in from Canada to be with us and she arrived that afternoon. She was able to stay with the kids while I went to visit Scott.

Shirley said that she would accompany me again and we drove to the hospital together. Once I returned to the hospital, I felt relieved that my mom was there to take care of the kids.

The doctor met with me again and discussed the tests that they intended to perform that day. They gave me an hour to spend with Scott. Every time I had to walk through those doors, I felt resistance. It was very traumatic and I felt scared. I didn't like what was in front of me. Seeing Scott like this was hard and I thank God that my children did not see him like this. They held onto the memories of him snorkeling in Lanai. I lay beside Scott and talked to him.

I also had Shirley with me, being my rock. I am still in awe of her strength and her willingness to be in the room with us. I had always known her to be a strong and smart woman. She is exactly who I needed by my side.

## Saturday, March 12, 2022

Many offered to fly to be by our side but I didn't know what we needed. All I wanted was to have my children close and to cry.

I thought about how I will never be able to remove their pain. They did not deserve this immense trauma, which shattered them to their very cores.

I had not slept in days. I had already called my immediate family. I could barely speak without bawling. I could barely talk at all. I had to *find* time to call people, because my main focus was being there for my kids. I would wait until Sophia and Matéas fell asleep before calling people, or I would text people. Who wants to announce this news by text? But at times, this was my reality.

Nobody wanted to go outside, but I knew staying inside watching movies was also not the solution. I told the kids to get their swimsuits on and we went to the pool.

I looked around and everyone was smiling, enjoying their vacation and the beauty of Maui. I felt like I was in a different realm, floating in a nightmare. I thought, *is this what depression feels like?*

I swam with the kids and sensed we had all gotten into a meditative state. We quieted our minds and that liberated us. I saw my children smile underwater and that gave me hope.

Once again, Shirley drove me to the hospital. At the hospital, the doctor explained that I would have to start thinking about what I wanted to do about keeping Scott on life support. The doctor told me that the process of taking Scott off life support could be planned for the next day. I did not feel comfortable making this decision alone and told the doctor that I had to call Scott's mother and stepmother.

Later, I was introduced to an organ-donation coordinator who asked about the medications Scott was on. He said that the dose of Scott's antidepressant was very high and if Scott had not been consistent in taking it, that could have created these large spikes of highs and lows. Once the coordinator was gone, I lay down with Scott again and talked to him.

In the evening, I called family members and asked them what they thought we should do. They all agreed that this is not how Scott would want to live: brain-dead and kept alive with machines. I could not sleep and dreaded sitting by during the process the next day, but I knew removing Scott from life support was the right choice.

## Sunday, March 13, 2022

I was told to arrive at the hospital at 11 a.m. to start the process. At 10 a.m. Shirley and I left for the hospital. At 10:13 a.m. my cell phone rang and the doctor informed me that Scott had just died on his own. An overwhelming sense of relief rushed over me. I did not want to lay beside him as they removed all the machines. I had been so scared. This was a big weight taken off my shoulders.

When we entered the room, I noticed a significant change in Scott's features. His skin was pale and drooping. They gave me some space and time on my own to spend with him. I played his favorite song from The Cure, "Lovesong." I said everything that I needed to say to him and then said my final goodbye. Walking out of that hospital was the strangest feeling. Was this my reality or just a nightmare? I had to go back and tell my kids that their father had died and he was never coming back.

Once I was back at the condo, I told my kids. We cried and held each other. How do you explain suicide to a six- and eight-year-old? The hospital suggested using the analogy "brain illness." I liked that analogy and it was true. He hurt himself because of his brain illness. That was the truth and they deserved the truth.

After a little while, I said, "Let's go to the beach and run into the ocean." They loved that idea. It sounded like a good release for all of us from all the pain.

Our family friends met us and my mom on the beach. We ran into the ocean holding hands and we went under water to hear the whales sing. That was our favorite thing to do. It felt peaceful underwater. Matéas popped his head up out of the water and said "Maman, if Dad died because he was sad to lose his dad, then now I want to die because I lost mine." It was like being stabbed in the heart. I quickly held him in my arms and said "NO! This is not how you ever deal with sadness. God loves you, and I love you with all my heart!"

This is the one of many reasons I want to seek all the tools available for mental health. I want to read and learn from others who have been in the dark and got out. What did they do differently? I need to learn so that I can teach my kids and change the generational line of suicide in the family. This needs to stop now and I will dedicate my life to fighting for mental health awareness.

**Monday, March 14, 2022**

I felt paralyzed as to what to do next. I had not slept since March 10th. I knew that I had to write a message to everyone to let them know that Scott had passed away. I also had to write an obituary. I cried a lot with my children, trying to answer their questions the best I could. My children knew Dad had been sad and they had seen his struggles. There was some understanding but it was all too much for everyone. We were now all very sad, just like Dad. We watched movies to break away from our reality. I also made sure that we went outside and swam. I knew staying in all day would not benefit us. I didn't feel like getting out of bed, but I did. I was numb and in shock.

Then the question arose: when should we go back to Alaska? I dreaded going home without Scott, entering our home without him, facing my new reality without my partner. I froze and did not book any flights.

## Tuesday, March 15, 2022

It was 3 a.m. when I began writing my message for our dental office Facebook page. This was my new reality and I had to take on all responsibilities from now on. That weight felt heavy but at times, mostly on that early morning, I had a wave of energy.

Later that morning, a very good friend called and asked if she could help with booking our flights. Normally I would've said no and that I got it, but this time, I felt relieved that someone offered because this was the thing that I was avoiding and dreading the most: going home. With her husband's help, my friend booked our flight to Alaska for March 17. We had to get back for the kids' sakes. They needed to be around their friends and go back to school.

## Wednesday, March 16, 2022

The hardest thing to do after you lose someone is to go through their things. When we started to pack our suitcases, the kids wanted to bring home everything that had belonged to their dad and not throw anything away. My mom stayed with the kids while I went back to our condo to pack. I grabbed Scott's suitcase and I started collecting his clothing from the drawers and closets. I could smell him and could not believe he was gone. I picked up a worn shirt, brought it to my nose, and smelled it. His scent made me feel like he was still there with me. Tears poured down my cheeks and I lost it. I cried out loud. I did not feel like packing; it was just too hard. I lay down on the bed and cried.

After a few minutes, I took a deep breath and got back up, telling myself that I could do this. I turned on some music because music has always been very healing for me. I packed all of his jiujitsu gear because it was something he had enjoyed and I knew our kids would someday want to see the gear again. I checked inside his travel bag and there were about a dozen pharmaceutical bottles and two large knuckle knives. I called a friend who is a fire chief and asked how to properly dispose of pharmaceuticals. I was not going to bring them home. I was able to give them to the detective that had interviewed me.

I looked around and knew we would never be back in our Maui condo. This was a place we loved coming to with family and friends. My mom and stepfather had renovated this condo for Scott and his brother. They had purchased this condo years before we got married. We had come at least twice a year to escape the long, dark winters of Alaska. All the fun memories here were over. This would not be our paradise getaway any longer. I locked our closets and lay down on the bed again, feeling completely drained. Later, I packed Scott's travel guitar, travel bag, and suitcase. I walked out of the condo and was relieved that task was over.

**Thursday, March 17, 2022**

In the morning, my mom helped everyone get ready to go to the airport. My mother was flying home to Alaska with us. Sophia and Matéas were excited to return to their friends. While we were checking in at the airport, everything seemed so strange without Scott. It just felt wrong, empty, like we had forgotten something. We got on the plane and the flight attendants were extremely caring with all of us. A dear friend had called the airlines to tell them that we were flying home after this tragic event. The flight attendants gave the kids things to color, wings, chocolate, and a kids snack pack. They truly made all of us feel loved. My kids watched their movies on their tablet and traveled well, as usual.

We landed in Alaska and walked to the escalator. As we descended, we were surprised to see many of our friends with our dog, Rose Bud. Our friends were holding flowers, teddies, and gift baskets. My kids and I fell into their arms while tears rolled down our faces. Their hugs were comforting and loving. It was the most beautiful surprise to see them all there. I loved how they had picked up our dog from the kennel and brought her to the airport. The kids were thrilled to see Rose Bud. That brought them so much comfort. I never asked anyone to come pick us up. I had my vehicle at the airport, but I also knew my car would probably not start since it had been sitting there for almost three weeks in the freezing cold. I had had issues with my car often and this had happened to me several times coming back from a trip.

My car did not start, but luckily, our friends were there to help. We jumped my car and it finally started. We all drove to my home together in a caravan. Nonetheless, the one thing I dreaded the most was about to happen: I was going to walk into our home knowing that Scott was never going to walk through those doors again.

When I reached my home I saw two cars parked in front of my house. We walked in and saw that many of our friends and their children were there, ready to make our entrance less painful. Friendly children came running to my kids with open arms. More hugs from everyone. I saw a friend cooking in the kitchen. All I could feel was an outpouring of love coming from everyone. Again, I never asked any of them to do this, but they just knew that we needed it.

I know it was not easy for anyone to stay strong for us. They were all in shock and grief as well. They loved Scott too. They showed up and truly went above and beyond. It was the arrival that set the tone for our healing at home. We would not be alone and we would have a community to watch over us. I appreciated seeing all our friends there. My kids were smiling with their friends. They were elated to see them. I knew how important it was for them to have friends to lift them up too, safe friends to talk to and share their emotions with.

I did call the parents of my kids' best friends and warn them that my kids may talk about the event with their children. I wanted them to be able to prepare their children to have hard conversations with my children. These friends will forever be whom my kids feel the most comfortable talking about their dad with. These friends knew Scott and what happened (as my children understood it).

I told my children the truth because I felt, and was told by mental health professionals, that it was best to use honesty. There are ways to explain this subject to kids at their age level. Sophia and Matéas knew what illness was since they had seen their grandfather suffer from terminal cancer. They saw their dad's darkness and had some understanding about depression. I had already talked about depression with them before Scott passed and explained that depression made him not think clearly.

# Chapter 6

# The Walls that Cave In

As the days advanced, I became more devastated. My name wasn't on any of Scott's bank accounts, and I had zero dollars in my bank account. Through the trauma of Scott's death, I couldn't fathom which step to take first.

The tasks were endless: payroll to pay for Scott's dental practice without access to his accounts; running the dental practice—did I want to? plan Scott's funeral; raise my two grieving children and manage the excruciating grief in my own heart.

I remember praying to God for guidance. No one had ever prepared me for this type of anguish, heartbreak, responsibility, and loss.

The walls of my life were caving and I felt paralyzed as they pressed into my living hell: a room without doors. The loneliness was unbearable.

Many times in my life when I didn't have a solution to my problems, I pretended.

I pretended I was happy, even when I was sad. I pretended all was well, even when I felt crazy. I pretended most when my dreams had been stolen.

I sat feeling the depths of emotional suffocation as the burdens piled up on my shoulders. I felt overwhelmed, scared, and stripped of my power. I remember days when all I could feel was small, worthless, and not good enough. I know. I know how being stuck can feel.

At this time, after Scott died, I didn't pretend. I had nothing left. The tank was empty and the only way forward was walking step-by-step upon the foundation of my truth. I felt it all. Painful, excruciating, and in this dark pain, there was newness. I had never done this before.

As little by little I stepped away from the pretending, I began to let go. I started to share. I shared about Scott, his death, and our feelings—my children's and mine. I began to live in my truth while the fear was real, even palpable at times. The fear of how to manage our finances, run a dental office, learn how to make decisions that I had never had to make before.

As I began to pray for help, miracles started to happen.

The first miracle was the friends that greeted us at the airport with our dog and with a sign bearing our name. I never asked them for that. We arrived at our home and it was spotless and there was food in the refrigerator. My children's best friends arrived shortly after we did, with arms wide open to embrace my children and their pain. God sent these friends as angels. He knew what we needed to be able to step into our home for the first time with no Scott, with just his suitcase containing his things.

The first miracle flowed into the next: a meal train, GoFundMe, house cleaning services. The love that was poured into our family was just a reflection of the impact Scott had had on everyone.

When I did not know how I would pay our mortgage, the lawsuit lawyers, the bills that were piling up, friends and family members sent large donations because they knew I had no access to income or money at this time. This was intensely uncomfortable for me because I was not used to receiving and no one wanted anything in return. They just wanted me to not have to worry about one more thing. I will never forget the relief that I felt and the weight that was lifted off my shoulders. I love that I can now give back to others who are in a similar financial situation because someone did that for me. Pay it forward, as they say.

We celebrated Scott's life at the Methven family vineyard in Oregon in June of 2022. The skies were covered in clouds and it poured so hard that we felt Scott wanted us to know he was there. During the celebration, friends and family spoke of their love for Scott. Tears, rain, and sweat all mixed together as I listened to the stories of Scott's life being shared. As the final speech ended, the rain subsided and two rainbows appeared. My daughter looked up at the sky and said, "My dad did that." We all felt it to be true. It was one rainbow for Scott and one for his father, who had passed away the day after Scott. They were both showing us that they were here with us and sending us their love.

The next miracle was all the synchronicities that came together with ease for my family and me to move to Arizona a few months after Scott passed.

It took a deep well of resilience to come to see these miracles. The time I spent suppressing the miracle that was my life prevented me from seeing the consistent, daily depression I was experiencing.

# Chapter 7

# The Grip of Depression

Depression is a form of numbing our truth. We numb ourselves from the truth by the disillusionment of the good days.

It's in the disillusionment of the good days that we lie to ourselves. In lying, we refuse to see the truth.

So we choose the illusion.

An illusion, by definition, is something that deceives by producing a false or misleading impression of reality.

Depression is a type of illusion that we start to live into.

When you think of the word depression do you automatically visualize someone curled on the floor crying, someone who is in bed for weeks not wanting to get up?

Do you believe that if someone isn't depressed one day that they aren't in danger the next?

Scott was struggling in a deep depression. He was also getting up five days a week to manage, lead, and practice in his dental office. I loved working with Scott as his dental hygienist. I would see him smile at patients, talk and share stories, while also empathizing with their pain and concerns. He would joke with his patients, putting them at ease. Laughter, which was uncommon at home, was a consistent sound in our dental office. He could brighten a room just by being in it.

After work, Scott would come home and, with his shoulders slumped, walk to his room, exhausted from his day. The brightness he used to carry in his work was merely a dull light in our home. He would immediately get on his phone and focus on emails from lawyers and investigators. Scott was being sued and he had hired investigators to prove that he was wronged by the plaintiffs. He wanted the truth to be told and he worked tirelessly with an investigator to find evidence. He *did* find evidence, but with the Covid shutdown and the backlog of court cases piling up, the truth was never brought to the surface. His mood changed as he became immersed in this battle. It became an obsession and a distraction. He was unable to be present at home with me and the kids and he soon became a hollow shell. *We could see him, but we could not feel him.*

When he came home, I would be in the kitchen preparing dinner and taking care of our kids. My desire for him to *see* me was never met. I ached for him to look at me or talk to me. He ignored me and I could feel myself slowly falling into depression. I had a sign hanging in my kitchen that held my favorite quote by Wayne Dyer: "Change your thoughts, change your life."[1]

I read this quote many times, every day, allowing the words to help lift me from the sinking sands of depression. Many of

---

[1] Wayne Dyer, *Change Your Thoughts—Change Your Life: Living the Wisdom of the Tao,*" (Carlsbad: Hay House, 2009).

my friends said that I was changing, that I felt different to them. I would say in my mind, *we have a roof over our heads, our kids are healthy, we have wonderful friends and family. We have more than most.*

I needed to focus on the good that we had. Being grateful saved me from leaning into Scott's darkness. Even though I felt lonely raising our kids, I would keep my mind always focused on finding the good.

Regardless of my focus and my desire to pull my mental state out of depression, my situation didn't change. Each day, my husband would work, come home, lie down on his bed, and be on his phone while drinking heavily and using pharmaceutical drugs.

I stopped asking for help from Scott because when I asked, he would get mad at me and yell in front of the kids. I quickly learned to keep the peace and to stay quiet or risk getting his normal response: "I work five days a week. This court case is very important and we could lose everything."

Many might assume that the lawsuit caused Scott to spiral into depression. Though it was a huge contributor, it wasn't the only factor. Scott had created a toxic internal environment. He had never dealt with his on-and-off relationship with his mother. This was related to an abandonment trauma from Scott's childhood that he had suppressed and avoided at all cost. When I met Scott, he had not spoken to his mother in years. This was hard for me to comprehend because I am so close to my own mother.

Scott was also taking opioids to numb both his back pain and internal suffering. For a year before his death, he was drinking every day in addition to taking pain meds and antidepressants. So when more toxicity came in through the lawsuit, he was already broken.

Scott was like a house that has termites eating away at it for years. During our 16 years together, Scott's daily choices, bit by bit, destroyed his soul. His consistent use of prescription pills and his overdrinking created holes inside of him, like the house that had been eaten by insects. So, when the lawsuit hit, he crumbled and fell deeper into depression.

For outsiders, he hid his depression behind large smiles, jokes, and his brightness that faded when he entered our home. His depression was rarely seen by anyone outside our family.

The truth was, we were both in depression. My depression was brought on by my constant suppression while his depression was brought on by his actions, external pressures, and internal environment.

Depression is not what we always imagine and seldomly affects only one spouse. If one has experienced it, then the other has most likely also battled it in their own way.

# Chapter 8

# **Environment Matters**

Not only can our physical environment be damaged—with the things we put INTO our bodies, or the things we watch and listen to—*but the environment of our minds can also be damaging.*

It is too easy to get stuck in the mud within the mind. The negative self-talk such as:

*I did it wrong;*
*I am the problem;*
*I will never be enough;*
*Everyone would be so much better without me;*
*I am a horrible friend.;*
*Why am I always making mistakes or messing things up?;*
*I hate myself;*
*I can never do it right,* and other phrases can find their way into our minds and are as toxic as drinking poison.

I witnessed this train of thought eating away at Scott. His environment, both physical and mental, was poisonous.

The years of him taking prescription pills had created toxicity within his body and had taken over his mind. Toward the end of his life, he was taking an antidepressant in high doses and combined that with overdrinking alcohol.

Now that I have spoken up about his suicide publicly, I have had many people tell me that they experienced suicidal ideation when they took an antidepressant. It's even advertised as a warning on some antidepressant manufacturers' TV commercials! Since Scott never once mentioned that he had suicidal ideation, I was not aware of his inner battle. I asked him over and over if he had any such thoughts as I could see him deteriorating, but he always assured me that he did not.

Now that I am aware of the effects of antidepressants (keep in mind that I cannot name a particular brand, but some are worse than others), especially when combined with alcohol, I would suggest people think twice about using these prescriptions. Mind you, if you are already on these prescriptions, please seek the advice of a medical professional before ceasing your medication. I believe antidepressants may save lives, but I also think they should be used in conjunction with seeking the root cause of your problems.

I know that Scott would never choose to take his life, not from his truest self—the Scott that I knew him to be, the one I loved and lived next to day-in-and-day-out. He was struggling big time. Life was hard for him. The grief of having to say his last goodbye to his father who was dying of cancer, the stresses of running a successful dental practice, and the lawsuit made his life unbearable. He experienced intense physical back pain from working as a dentist in a hunched position for over eight hours a day, five to six days a week. His pain was so high that he needed to numb it. He didn't have the tools to help him manage his pain, but he also didn't choose to learn about the tools he could have used. He refused to go to therapy, thus closing the doors on his ability to heal from the wounds that had created such deep pain within him.

This was the most painful part for me: his unwillingness to ask for help so he could heal, so he could find a new path, a better way. The darkness that had overcome him was so heavy that he felt that he could not escape it. The environment within his mind and in his life was an impossible hole that he was eventually unable to climb out of. The deep love and connection we had could not close the gap of his depression. He felt nothing could get him out. This was so grievous for me because Scott was a happy person by nature. He had a beautiful heart and bright soul, but his choice to combine 10 different prescription pills with overdrinking alcohol and isolating from his friends and family created the toxic cocktail that I believe led to his death.

**Our environment matters.**

Our environment can be the thing that tips us or catches us. I know that Scott was here to accomplish great things. His spirit was bright, his heart was huge, and his soul ached to serve, but the environment in which he chose to live rotted away his spirit and closed down his heart. He was no longer able to connect with or see his family. His focus had turned inward, and with that, the environment he built in his mind became infected. His self-hate and self destructive thoughts led to his external environment getting more and more poisonous. His drug use spiraled into wild benders. He had multiple needles lying around in his room at all times; he used them for injections of pain killers for his back pain and for testosterone. What once would've alarmed him and disgusted him became his everyday norm.

Toward the end, we had to sleep in different rooms because I no longer felt safe sleeping with him. His room had become a cave of darkness. I would walk by it and feel the pain and suffering that came from within. He would come home and seclude himself inside his room, only coming out once we had all gone to bed.

I was lost on what to do for him. I begged him to get help. I found a healing facility in California that helped with drug addictions, but he refused to go. I prayed every day for him and was always trying to ease his stress in whatever way I could. I took on all the duties with the kids and the house and I would work at the office as a dental hygienist and organize staff events. I tried not to complain that I was tired of doing everything alone. I saw our kids yearning for their dad to play with them or to sit with us for some family time.

Ultimately, the environment and life he chose was up to him. Each brick he laid and every action he took led him to not have the ability to fight any longer.

The darkness prevailed with Scott. His environment opened the door to a fury of depression.

This didn't happen overnight. This was a progression in his environment and with his daily actions.

Scott's staff and I noticed that whenever October came, as the days got shorter and shorter with the winter coming, Scott's mood would change. In December the sun would rise at 9:30 a.m. and set at 3 p.m. Since Scott worked from 9 a.m. to 5 p.m. he would not get any time in the daylight before or after work.

Seasonal Affective Disorder (SAD) is very prevalent in Alaska and we saw it with many people that could not travel outside of Alaska in the winter. Most years, our winters lasted from October to May.

When the summer months finally arrived in Alaska, they were often filled with clouds and rain. In my 16 years of living there, I could count on one hand how many sunny and warm summers we had. Additionally, getting a full night of sleep during the summer months was challenging because the extended daylight could last up to 24 hours. I vividly recall the insomnia I experienced during my first summer there when the sun never truly set and it really only got dusky. My belief is that this continuous daylight probably created a dysregulated circadian rhythm for most of the year in many people living in Alaska. I personally observed higher instances of depression in Alaska in the office and grocery store, and among friends and family.

*The environment of Alaska was not ideal for Scott to fully thrive in his profession and his personal life.*

Scott usually worked five to six days a week because he was burdened by $500,000 in student loans and was over $1 million in debt from building his dental practice. The constant pressure to overproduce in order to cover overhead costs was a major stressor. Managing two to three dental hygienists meant Scott was sometimes seeing up to 50 patients a day. Many patients held fear or dislike for dentists, and Scott heard daily comments from patients about how much they hated the dentist. Scott would have to suppress his emotional response to such remarks so he could continue to perform his role as a dentist and retain patients.

As a dentist, Scott not only dealt with the physical demands of dentistry, causing pain in his neck and back from being hunched over all day, but also willingly took on the emotional stress and the past dental trauma of his patients. Feeling guilty about the cost of dentistry, he often gave away his time for free. The pressure to perform, please everyone, alleviate fear, and run the office was extremely exhausting. Despite his day officially ending at 5 p.m., being a practice owner meant there were always other things to handle, so Scott often brought some of his work home. Or he worked on the weekends for emergency calls that required his attention.

Imagine if he no longer enjoyed practicing dentistry? He loved what he did, but he also felt stuck. He would often dream of relocating and working as an associate for two to three days a week or exploring teaching, especially given his expertise in root canals. Many dentists share similar points of view, expressing dissatisfaction with their profession and feeling trapped. Unlike other professions like medicine or law, where individuals can shift to different departments or specialties, dentists often find themselves limited by their training and schooling, lacking alternative options within their field.

From the 40+ hours of hunching over patients every single week for years on end, Scott continued to have immense back pain, which meant that he had no motivation to stay active. He began taking pain medication and muscle relaxers to relieve his pain. On the weekends he drank more heavily and slept all day. This cycle continued for years.

The environment of his job was not conducive to his overall health.

After being in practice for seven years as the sole owner, just as he was beginning to achieve financial success and was finally able to consider working fewer days a week, Scott faced a lawsuit. Unfortunately, he had to continue working five to six days a week to cover legal fees and fight for what he believed was the truth. While I also believed he was wronged, we couldn't prove it within our legal system. This battle stretched over seven years and involved multiple lawyers, computer forensics, the FBI, and the police. It became an obsession to prove his innocence, ultimately destroying our entire family dynamic. The conflict, driven by money and the desire to be proven right, took a toll on all of us, impacting our well-being.

The environment of the lawsuit, the courts, and all that was involved created more toxicity and harm in Scott's life.

Throughout this challenging period, one thing that provided solace for Scott was finding a dental community that listened to him and offered support. It was a group of like-minded individuals, a support network for navigating the challenges in dentistry. This association is called The American Academy of Clear Aligners (AACA). Witnessing his experience in this association, I saw hope in him. It was in this environment that he regained his happiness, and his passion for dentistry resurfaced. In this community, he could share his gifts, and I encouraged him to attend conferences for further engagement and community.

This new group was a huge blessing for him and our family.

I pleaded with him to stop drinking, quit using opioids, and move us all away from the long dark winters.

Feeling stuck in his life, Scott suppressed his deepest desires and by doing so stayed in the environments that led to his life of depression and numbing.

We all have the ability to choose our environments. You may feel like you are stuck in your predicament but if it is creating toxicity and harm to you in any way, choose something different.

You have the gift of choice even when you believe you are stuck. There is always a way out. Choose to place yourself in a position that will fuel you, fulfill you, and nurture you.

Suicide is not a decision that is made overnight. It is one that is formed from the compound effect of negativity, unhealed wounds, and suppressing the desire to get out of being stuck.

Change your environment, and watch your life change.

# Chapter 9

# The Waves of
# Guilt and Shame

Suicide creates a ripple effect of guilt and shame for the loved ones of those who took their own life. If you are reading this and you feel like your family is better off without you and dying is the answer, please know you have other options. Our world will be far better off if you call just one person and tell them that you are not okay, that you are experiencing suicidal thoughts and thinking about leaving. Reaching out, the bravest act you can take, will open the first door toward the light. There are many healing modalities available and doing the work will leave a legacy of strength and courage for your family and the world.

*But departing from your family by suicide leaves them in a wave of destruction.*

On the day Scott passed away in the hospital, I had the impossible task of explaining to my children that their dad had died, which led to numerous questions. *How did he hurt himself? Why did he hurt himself? What are we going to do without him?*

**The devastation for our family is still unexplainable.**

Suicide leaves those you love in a drowning mess of guilt and shame. Losing a loved one will always be full of pain and grief. This is natural and extremely hard, but losing a loved one to death by suicide leaves those left behind with not only pain and grief but also guilt and shame. This shame will swallow them whole: shame that they didn't know you were struggling that badly; shame that they failed you; shame that somehow they weren't enough for you to stay.

The shame that I felt was often from the projection of other people's shame. Many expressed their shame of not having done enough. I also remember hearing people's insinuations. I could feel them wondering if *I* could have done something differently. So many people wondered why *I* hadn't been able to save him. While these insinuations were inaccurate, my environment was quite destructive.

This is a pressure no one should ever have to go through. The guilt that you didn't do enough to save someone's life is far too great for someone to carry.

I do carry it. My children carry it. Scott's friends and family members carry it.

The burden of "Did I do enough? Was there something MORE I could've done?" is a heavy one to bear.

The truth is, there was nothing we could have done. I begged Scott for years to get help. *He refused.* I found healing facilities, therapists, groups, books . . . anything that may have been the support he was so deeply needing, but he always refused.

This is where we get to honor each person having their own ability to choose. Though what Scott did would have never been what *I* would have chosen for him, it is ultimately what *he* chose and I had to come to peace with that.

## To Those Who Struggle with Suicide Ideation

I am writing this for those of you who might be considering suicide. Whatever thoughts you might have, **DON'T believe them.**

Your family will **NOT** be better without you.
You are not alone in your pain and isolation.
Your feelings are not **TOO MUCH.**
*You* are not too much.
You are worthy of living.
Your life is worth creating.
You are never stuck. Even when you think that you are, there is always a solution.

Death **IS NOT** the solution.

## Choose to live.

Life may feel very hard right now, but the hard will pass.

Reach out. Find someone you can talk to. If you don't have anyone, call the National Suicide Hotline today at 988. You can call them as many times as you want, every single day. Don't suppress your feelings. Talk about them and let them leave you. Speak them out to someone. Fight to live.

I am inviting you to choose life.

No matter what your mind tells you, your family and the world will NOT be better without you. The guilt and shame *they* will feel in the aftermath of your death will destroy them. The guilt that others will place on them will be felt for years.

Do not believe the lies that are playing in your mind. I know that they may seem too heavy to fight off, but they are not you. They are not true.

You are needed in this world and there is help for you.

**A Letter To Those Who Have Lost a Loved One By Suicide**

*Dear friend,*

*Every time I hear the news of someone dying by suicide, I instantly feel the excruciating pain that my children and I felt on that dreadful day. I get full-body chills and I want to cry. I don't know you, but I can feel you. I just want to drive over to you and hold you in my arms. Cry with you and hold your pain with you. We have this invisible connection and I see you. The bond of being family members of suicide is a bond we never wanted, but now we are in this community together. Only we will know the truth and the impact it has on our entire body and lifetime. Our connection needs no introduction. We just know the suffering and ripple effects. We can look into each other's eyes and have this inner knowing of the suffering we have gone* through. Everyone looks at you for all the answers and you feel you have to answer all of them to give them closure. We all know there will never be any closure and answers because the only person who could answer them best, has died. We must learn to let go and trust that this was their choice. Nobody could have changed the outcome except for that person, from within. What we can do is use our voices to share knowledge about mental health and suicide. Every story will be different, but I know in my heart that we can learn from each of them. It is okay to lose ourselves in the darkness sometimes, as long as we don't remain there too long. Never forget that there's always light to be found, so reach to open that door. My friend, it is time to take care of you and your heart. The physical pain in your heart will subside but you must reach out for healing. You cannot do this alone. If you start your healing journey and you have children, they too will learn from you. Their pain will also subside. It will come and go in waves and with each wave you will learn and grow. Do not drown in substance abuse or alcohol. Feeling will be torture at first but you will become more resilient as you incorporate healing modalities. I send you love. Know that I see you. May you find inner peace and calm in your journey.

Love,

Mélissa

## A Prayer of Hope

*Dear God,*

*I want help to hear your voice above all. Let hope lighten my darkness and empower me in the right direction. "I run to you, God: I run for dear life. Don't let me down!" (Psalms 31:1). "And hope does not put us to shame, because God's love has been poured out into our hearts through the Holy Spirit, who has been given to us" (Romans 5:5).*

*I surrender with my hands up in the air, praying that you fill my heart with hope and light. Help me trust your plan even when I cannot see the way. I am grateful for your love.*

*Amen,*

*Mélissa*

# Chapter 10

# **Rejection**

Rejection of our truth makes us angry. Rejection of our own voice makes us isolated. We fear others rejecting us but it is actually ourselves who do the rejecting.

Each time you silence your voice, you reject yourself.

Everytime you act small and insignificant, you reject yourself.

The suppression is the rejection.

We suppress our truths to make others feel better. The fear of our truth hurting another person is a big reason we push our truths down. We push them down like a garbage compactor, piling trash over trash, hoping that it will stay down, but like the garbage that eventually rises to the surface, so does our truth.

It will show up in our lives as rage and anger. It will rise as tears and outbursts. Or it will reveal itself in physical illnesses. The body will begin to show the wear and tear of those hidden truths.

I have watched this happen in real time in my life. The anger that seemed to take over me. The days of silently crying in the bathroom. The physical illness that screamed at me to pay attention.

These illnesses begged for me to pay attention to the truths that so deeply ached to be heard.

Suppressing was not something I started doing in my twenties or even my thirties. No, it began in my childhood. I vividly recall a moment when I was seven when my father, knowing I was emotional about saying goodbye, once again instructed me not to cry. It was a recurring ritual as I traveled from Vancouver, BC, to Quebec City to visit him every Christmas and summer. On that particular day at the airport, he made me promise to never cry again. In a stern voice, he emphasized that crying wasn't allowed when he dropped me off. Since that day, I trained myself to pretend I was happy, concealing the internal turmoil that wanted to break down in tears. Never again did I cry while saying goodbye.

This was the beginning of my suppression and the start of hiding my truth behind my smile. The pretending and the rejection of myself had started.

I knew my dad felt the heartache that I felt when I left. It hurt him as well and he too had created a shield to protect his heart. He did not want to feel this pain of saying goodbye. We often suppress our emotions because showing them is scary and is often viewed as weak, but in reality, showing our emotions is the strongest thing we could ever do. Expression is how we stay healthy.

From the young age of seven and until I was forty years old, I didn't know that. I was trained to suppress, to make others feel good and not worry about me. Hiding the truth behind my smile became a learned behavior to suppress my true feelings.

During Christmas break, I traveled back to Quebec as an unaccompanied minor. My stay typically involved residing with my grandmother on my dad's side and with my dad's sister. Christmas in Quebec was always festive and grandiose, filled with extended family and cousins. On Christmas Eve, we would gather together and, after the kids had a brief nap around 7 p.m., we would attend midnight mass. When we returned home, we enjoyed a large buffet, opened presents, and danced. The atmosphere was lively and enjoyable.

However, there were moments when I would hide in the bathroom and cry because I missed my mother, who had to stay in Vancouver for work over the holidays. After wiping away my tears, I would rejoin the party with a big smile. I didn't want anyone to feel sorry for me and I didn't want to dampen the festive atmosphere. I smiled to conceal my sadness.

I suppressed my sadness to make sure others were happy. I rejected my own inner feelings to make sure no one worried about me.

This was the beginning of this pattern for me. Suppress to please.

As I have chosen to speak my truth in all ways now, I realized that my smile is there when I am happy. I no longer feel like hiding my pain or truths. My smile is an outward expression of how I truly feel: **Happy.**

Many might wonder how I can be so happy after going through such tragedy and loss. I believe that as I share my truth, I am no longer suppressing. I am no longer rejecting myself and I am honestly grateful for all that I have, all of which results in authentic happiness.

When you see me smile from now on, you will know it is because I am happy.

# Chapter 11

# Ghosts of Generations

**M**y husband was emotionally unavailable. This wasn't his choice. He was disconnected because he was carrying the ghosts of his childhood wounds. I found that I was also repeating my own childhood patterns and reliving old wounds. As a young girl, my deepest desire was to receive my father's love. I was always doing whatever I could to please him in an effort to make him love me more. However, as an adult I never addressed my inner child, and that led me to attract similar patterns in my relationship with Scott.

My need to please and to suppress as a child carried over into my marriage. I suppressed my worries and concerns in an effort to have peace. This created bitterness inside my body that resulted in physical manifestations. It also contributed to the disconnection I experienced with Scott.

Scott carried childhood wounds of not feeling loved. These wounds were never addressed or healed. So with each new stressor that showed up in his life, these wounds got deeper and deeper, resulting in him being emotionally unavailable in our relationship and in our home.

On top of his own personal wounds, he had compounding effects that ran through his generational line. Within both sides of Scott's family there was death by suicide, a topic shrouded in silence and avoidance. The family chose not to speak of these, keeping them hushed and pushed under the rug. I remember knowing that there had been two deaths by suicide in Scott's family, but no one ever spoke of their lives or their deaths. It was almost as if they didn't speak about it, it didn't happen.

**This is the lie.**

Many think if we ignore suicide, it will go away. Like a disease that can be cured by avoidance, silence, and secrecy, many think speaking about suicide will cause contamination, so the silence continues. *We shouldn't talk about it*, but if we silence it, it will grow like a tumor in the body—unknown but slowly killing.

I refuse to participate in these beliefs any longer. I now confront the fear that this pattern might persist in my children or future generations. This is why I am deeply committed to igniting change and altering the trajectory of our family line by speaking about it.

I will never ignore the fact that Scott died by suicide. I will not silence it. I will not soften it or hide it. As painful as it can be, now I know this is the purpose of my life: suicide and mental health awareness. I will speak the truth and as I do so, I trust that it will clear our generational line of unresolved mental illness.

Trauma—especially suicide, addiction, and abuse—compound generationally, but we can be the driving force to ending the mental and physical damage. Trauma is like plaque on teeth. If you don't brush daily and get your bi-yearly cleaning, plaque builds up. With the buildup of plaque, cavities appear as the tooth begins to decay. It's the same with our generational line: If we don't do our own personal healing work, the "decay" may compound on each person within the family.

I cannot get my son's teeth cleaned for him. He must sit in that chair and get his own teeth cleaned. As it is with our healing work. I must do the work for myself and you must do the work for yourself. Each person in the generational line who chooses to do so cleans up the compounding trauma within the family line.

For my family's sake, I am addressing and healing my inner childhood wounds, coping with the loss of my husband, and overcoming the emotional and mental abuse I experienced. I am determined to find happiness and embrace the joys of this brief life with everyone around me. I am blessed with two healthy children, a wonderful family, and supportive friends. I cannot ask for more, and I am genuinely grateful.

I recognize that my happiness and the well-being of my children are my responsibility. Without putting in the hard work for personal growth and healing, no positive change can occur. It's through this dedication that my kids are smiling, finding the goodness in life, and feeling a sense of purpose to help others and provide hope.

Our generational trauma does not determine our future but it does affect us. We must be aware of what trauma has occurred within our lines and choose to heal. Heal our wounds. As we do so, we will clear out trauma to benefit our future generation. Be the voice that no longer hides the truth behind silence and closed doors. Be willing to look into the closet of your generations and do the work necessary to clean it up.

# Chapter 12

# My Journey with Suppression

Suppression is what I have known. Even though I did not have language for my words, behaviors, and actions, I was suppressing. When it showed up in my marriage, it didn't feel different to me. It actually felt comfortable, known, and sometimes friendly. It was my comfort zone. I was at ease with not having agency and suppressing to please others.

As Scott started to use prescription pills and overdrink alcohol, I had the urge to leave the marriage. I loved Scott so much but our relationship was falling apart. His addictions were destroying our lives. He no longer connected with me or the kids. I begged him to get help, but no matter the requests that I pleaded for, he refused to seek help, individually or together as a couple.

Unable to lead my life according to my own choices, I felt my power being stripped from me. I had to ask Scott for money and approval for every purchase. This made me feel suffocated, lonely, worthless, and small. I tiptoed around what I believed I deserved. Each month, Scott gave me an allowance that was not for me to go shopping for new clothes or go to a nearby spa. It was solely for our groceries and needs.

When I resumed working, the allowance that Scott gave me was discontinued, yet I still had to cover expenses like groceries, gas, and the children's needs. Saving enough money to leave the marriage became impossible. During a crisis with our new puppy, I faced a hefty $800 vet bill. Unable to call Scott for assistance, I reluctantly charged it to my credit card, deepening my financial burden. The despair of not being able to save money so I could escape weighed heavily on me.

My gut would churn with nervousness, making it difficult for me to eat. Over the years, my digestive system became increasingly intolerant to a variety of foods. Following some surgeries, I could only consume chicken broth because I had severe acid reflux. The impact was evident in significant weight loss, prompting concerned inquiries from those around me. Despite my struggles, I always wore a smile and assured everyone that I was fine.

My reluctance to speak out stemmed from a desire to not tarnish my husband's reputation, especially considering the deep admiration our small-town community held for Scott. I was concerned that revealing the truth might jeopardize his legal case, even though I believed he had been wronged and should've won the case.

Suppression slowly corroded me from within. The walls closed in and engulfed me. I constructed a façade, a lie encompassing my ultimate dream of a picture-perfect family. The belief that pretending to be happy would lead to genuine happiness proved false. Inside, I grappled with profound loneliness and sadness.

The stark contrast between my envisioned dream of an engaged, loving father for my children and the harsh reality left me despondent. Witnessing my kids yearning for a present and affectionate father, especially during moments when they observed other dads playing with *their* children, added to my sorrow. Sophia's tears reflected her longing for her dad's love, while Matéas internalized his pain, expressing it only occasionally through angry outbursts and slamming doors. The impact extended to all of us, with occasional outbursts of anger becoming a collective response to the underlying pain.

# Chapter 13

# The Cactuses
# are Calling

The realization that we needed to leave Alaska for Arizona was accompanied by a strong intuition urging me to make the move.

In September 2020, I flew to Quebec City to say my last goodbyes to my 93-year-old grandmother. My last conversation with her changed the trajectory of my life and nudged me toward my truth. She had shared how unmanaged stress had caused her to receive a breast cancer diagnosis in her 60s. She was able to survive this cancer but she said to "watch out for when your body is talking to you." This message propelled me to schedule a breast MRI once I returned to Alaska. My results showed a cyst and a ruptured silicone breast implant. In November 2020, I went to Arizona for my surgery to address the ruptured breast implant and to remove the cysts. I spent seven days in Arizona with my mother. This marked my first visit to that state. The difference between Alaska's freezing cold and dark conditions was a stark contrast to Arizona's sunshine. The sun in Arizona brought me a sense of warmth and joy. The vibrant atmosphere, beautiful restaurants, shops, hikes, and sunsets made a lasting impression. I felt a strong desire to make

Arizona my home, to escape the dark and prolonged winters of Alaska.

During my recovery period, I received excellent care and took the opportunity to rest, read, and engage in meaningful conversations with my mother. It was during these conversations that I opened up to her about the pain I was facing at home. My mother also shared a deep concern for Scott and, together, we sought ways to support him. Daily prayers were dedicated to our protection and a hope that Scott would recognize the goodness surrounding him.

Returning home after a week, I felt remarkably well. Surprisingly, I was no longer sore, and I didn't need any opioids for pain relief. I had consciously chosen to avoid opioids because I was aware of their potential to ensnare individuals into addiction. I had told my doctor that I did not want any of them and he reassured me that I did not need them. Opioids scared me because I saw how they held Scott captive.

It was a tremendous relief to discover that my cyst was benign and the ruptured implant had been successfully removed. Excited about the possibilities, I shared my enthusiasm for Arizona with Scott and suggested a potential move. However, he didn't share my excitement, expressing a dislike for the heat and the sun. Undeterred, during the night I found myself researching homes and schools in Arizona, discovering wonderful educational options for our kids and possible beautiful homes. I was hoping and dreaming for the life I desired, desperate to bring Scott and my children with me.

My curiosity led me to explore everything about Arizona, from hiking trails and restaurants to activities for kids. The prospect of endless fun and the ability to drive to other states rather than flying added to the appeal. However, I eventually questioned my obsession with Arizona, deeming it an unrealistic dream. I consciously stopped researching and suppressed this inspired dream. As I focused solely on Alaska and released my dream of an Arizona life, a part of me died

Concerned about the future education of our kids, I often discussed with Scott the idea of leaving Alaska before our children started middle school and high school. We were dissatisfied with the local options and concerned about substance abuse among the youth, as Alaska held the top rank in the U.S. for youth suicide rates.[2] Even routine trips to the grocery store exposed us to alarming situations. Scott agreed that moving before the kids reached middle school could be a good idea, with Texas often considered as a potential destination for us.

When Scott passed away, I figured we would move back to British Columbia, Canada. My mom lived there and I had many friends there. I started looking online for homes and schools in Kelowna, BC. Text messages between me and my friends in BC were filled with excitement and exchanges about potential homes to view, schools, and restaurants. I began imagining my new life there with the support of my friends and family. Then I started looking at Arizona for schools and homes. That dream would not leave me. I felt this

---

[2] America's Health Rankings, "Teen Suicide by State," data from CDC Wonder, Multiple Causes of Death Files, 2019–2021, https://www.americashealthrankings.org/explore/measures/teen_suicide/AK.

excitement inside and I remembered how much I loved Arizona.

The draw to research Arizona, and a knowingness that this was the best choice, became stronger. As I spoke my truth and told my friends, I received many responses like: who do you know there? Why Arizona? It's the desert and it is 120 degrees there in the summer.

The call to move to Arizona got stronger and no one understood why I was moving to that sunshiny state. A part of me didn't know either, but now I know: It was my calling.

My response to friends and family was simple: it was the strongest feeling that my heart and God sent me. It was a knowingness that it was indeed where we needed to live. I said that I would stay in Alaska for another year and then move. Nobody understood, but they supported my decision.

One month after Scott passed, my neighbor stopped by. I was rolling studded winter tires out of the garage to take pictures to sell them on the Internet. My neighbor asked if I was planning on moving. I told her that yes, eventually I would be moving. She then asked if I would accept an offer on my house right then. I paused and inside I knew I was ready to move but I worried that it would be too soon for my kids. I responded with "maybe" and she drove home. Soon after, her sister-in-law called and said she would like to purchase our house as is. I had already started thinking about how I'd have to paint, deal with repairs, and handle showings if I put my home on the market. This seemed too overwhelming for me at the time because my days were filled with dealing with lawyers, trying to manage the dental practice, piecing a puzzle together with Scott's finances, handling probate, paying bills, planning a celebration of life, helping my grieving children—and the list goes on. I had a daily list of tasks to tackle and putting my home on the market was not one I wanted to add. This offer seemed appealing, but still I was apprehensive. If I accepted her offer, I would have to move by July 14. That seemed impossible. How would I move while trying to do everything else?

A week later I received a formal offer for my house. I became ill that week and was vomiting. I remember trying to read the contract while lying by my toilet. I was so sick and exhausted. I felt a wave of nausea again and purged. I then grabbed my phone, took a deep breath, and decided to sign the offer. In my head I said *Screw it! I'm doing this!* I didn't want to be in Alaska anymore and I definitely didn't want to spend another dark, long winter by myself in this home, isolated on 50 acres in the dark.

This reality hit hard after that: My kids had never been to Arizona. How would this affect them?

I planned a quick, four-day trip to Arizona with my mom and kids. I booked our flights and hotel and emailed a realtor to request looking at a few homes while we were there.

We flew to Arizona and landed at sunrise. We looked out the airplane window and saw the beautiful pink hues in the sky peaking over the mountains. Driving to the hotel, we noticed the beautiful palm trees and cactuses. There was excitement but I still wondered if this was where we should move. I wished for clear signs. I took the kids to a water park, a dinosaur museum, and a butterfly museum and we swam at the hotel pool. The sun and warmth felt good, reenergizing, and healing.

On the third day in Arizona we went to see four homes in North Scottsdale. I was convinced North Scottsdale would be the best for us. We loved the mountains and we were used to mountain views. Our kids ran up to the first home and walked in. They looked at the kitchen and living room, then made their way to the bedrooms. Sophia announced that the master bedroom was hers. I looked back at her, smiled, and shook my head no. Did she really think this could be her room? I think so! I always felt like she was an old soul and seemed much older than her age. In each home, Matéas would pick his room and my mom would pick her room. I was surprised by how much my kids enjoyed looking at homes. They were smiling and laughing.

My mom was also excited to possibly live somewhere warm all year long. We still didn't know when she would get her green card. We had applied four years before and had still not heard when she would get an interview. There was hope of the possibility. It had always been my dream to have my mother living close to us. Our kids were so close to their grandmother and we did not have any family in Alaska that supported us. My entire family was in Canada and most of Scott's family lived in Oregon.

We walked into the third home and the kids raced to find each of their bedrooms first. I loved the backyard with a pool, outdoor living space, and a view of the mountains. My mom loved the fireplace, details in the kitchen, and outdoor living. She had created two bed and breakfast resorts in Canada and was excellent at noticing the potential for homes. I could tell she loved this home too.

Near this home there was a bike path to a nearby school. I felt excited but was still not 100% sure this was *the* home. I wanted to feel like, *this is it,* but I was not as confident about this choice as my mother was. It *was* our first choice though, and I told the realtor that we may be interested in putting in an offer. It seemed a strange coincidence that the owner's husband had died unexpectedly and she wanted to move. I saw this as a possible sign.

We flew back to Alaska and I hesitated to put an offer on the home. I knew the market was tough and you had to be quick to put an offer. My realtor called and said someone else would be putting in an offer by 5 p.m. and if I was still interested, I should put in an offer as well. I still didn't know but at this point, I had to find a home fairly quickly. I put an offer on this home in North Scottsdale. The owner had two offers by then and I thought that, knowing my situation, she would choose me.

My realtor called me a day later and said that the owner had chosen the other family. I took a deep breath and wondered why I had taken so long to put in an offer. I messed up our opportunity. Everyone loved this home. I was sad and discouraged. It was all so overwhelming. So many big decisions were on my shoulders. I felt drained. How could I make clear decisions right then?

I had the celebration of life coming up in June and I had no time to go back to Arizona. I just kept looking at homes online and emailing schools. I felt it was extremely hard to search from afar. You can't feel the home, the neighborhood, the schools. It was just pictures and some reviews for the schools. I thought, well maybe I'll rent a home first. Rent seemed to be the same cost as a mortgage payment, though.

As the day of the celebration of life approached, I felt more and more nervous and could not concentrate on anything but the celebration of life. I needed to write my speech and wondered if I would be able to speak in front of everyone. I had decided to do the celebration in Oregon at Scott's father's vineyard. Scott's dad passed one day after Scott and the celebration of life for Scott's dad would be the day before Scott's celebration of life. They both had many common friends that would be at both events. I thought having their celebrations of life one day after the next would make it easier for most. Scott always loved going to his father's home and winery. It was a special place for us.

The week before the celebration of life, I went to the funeral for my dear friend's father. I wanted to be there for her and her family. They were all like family to us in Alaska and I loved them very much.

I walked into the church, and I could see my friend's mom greeting people. I thought to myself, this will be me in a week. I put my arms around her mother and tears started flowing down my cheeks. Tears flowed heavily and I began crying uncontrollably. I felt embarrassed and walked away. I was supposed to be there to support and strengthen *her* family. I sat in the church and tried to calm down. That took me a good five to ten minutes. I could not stop the tears. Friends came to sit beside me and they rubbed my back as everyone was singing the beautiful church songs. I could not sing. Tears threatened to come out. It was a beautiful celebration and I was able to stay strong for the second half of it.

I went home and thought about Scott's upcoming funeral. I realized I might be a mess and not able to talk. I finished writing my speech. How would my kids be feeling at the event? It would be overwhelming for them too. How about creating a calming corner for the kids for that day? A place they could retreat to and feel safe. I bought a white tent and inflatable furniture. My sister-in-law, who lives in Oregon, helped fill this tent with crafts and teddies. This was the best decision ever for our kids. They used it for both celebrations. It did get to be too much with so many people and this was a great retreat for them to go to with their cousins and friends.

The day of Scott's father's celebration of life, we were all nervous, but as a family we all supported each other. We had Scott's stepbrothers, stepsister, and their significant others and their children. I knew that I would also see one of Scott's brothers whom Scott had not spoken to in years. I know to always lead with love and compassion and taught that to my kids. You always rise when you lead with love instead of hatred.

As that brother walked in with his wife and kids, I wondered if they would come and say hello. They did not. My daughter ran to me and said, "Mom, I saw my uncle. Can I go say hi?" "Of course! Let's go," I replied. On our way over, I ended up getting tangled in a conversation with someone else and Sophia decided not to wait. She walked over there by herself. She ran back to me and said, "Mom, I did it! I said hi to my uncle." She felt proud and was happy to see him. I think he reminded her of her dad. I loved that about her and felt proud.

She just went with her heart and did not overthink it. She didn't let fear take her over.

She then told me that she wanted to ask him to come tomorrow to her dad's celebration of life. He had not responded to the RSVP, but I said okay and was very impressed with Sophia's strength. From afar, I watched her ask and run back to me. I looked in her eyes and could tell she was holding in tears. I gave her a big hug knowing what the answer had been. I told her that it was probably too hard emotionally. She still could not understand. It just did not make sense to her. She had a brother and she could not grasp the idea.

At the end of my father-in-law's celebration of life, I walked over to Scott's brother and said hi. It felt good to just let everything go.

Too much damage had been done. So much pain and suffering in the entire family who had lost two incredible men in their lives in just two days. It was just all too much. I wanted the egos and masks to come off.

That was the last time I saw Scott's brother and his family. Once I moved, I had to concentrate on our healing and I needed space to do so. I learned to process the pain and hurt. I now pray for them and send them love and light. Letting go was the best step for my healing, but it also took time and a lot of dedication. I also have compassion for their pain.

The next day, the day of Scott's celebration of life, we spent the morning setting up. Before the guests arrived, I was feeling overwhelmed and worried about all the details, so I had to retreat for a few minutes. I had to let go and trust that everything would go well. My friend touched up my hair and said "I'm proud of you for walking away when you felt it was too much." It was good to hear that and helped me feel calmer and ready to go greet everyone. I was excited to see my family that flew from Quebec City, friends from Canada that I had not seen for a while, and all of Scott's wonderful friends and family. Everyone's presence created a loving energy.

A downpour started, but luckily we had tents. I definitely felt this was Scott wanting to be heard. He wanted to let us know that he was there with us. We could barely hear the pastor give his speech because the rain was so loud. I knew that I was next to speak. I walked over to the podium with Sophia and Matéas beside me. They stood there as I read my speech. All of a sudden the rain subsided. Thinking back to how I had reacted the previous week at the funeral in Alaska, I was surprised at how calm I felt speaking in front of everyone without ever breaking down. Sophia wanted to speak as well and had written a little speech. I finished speaking and allowed her to be at the podium for her turn. Matéas and I stood next to her. She spoke clearly and with confidence. I was very impressed and in awe of her strength again. Matéas was only six years old and chose not to speak in front of everyone.

We sat down and listened to all the other beautiful speeches. I still wish that I would have hired a videographer to capture all the speeches and events. My kids loved hearing all the fun and loving stories about their dad. The sun was peeking through the clouds now.

As I continued to listen to the speeches, once in a while Matéas would leave for the calming tent and to play with friends. He was dressed in a light blue suit with a white dress shirt and white shoes. As we all listened to someone speak, a little voice said "I'm sorry maman." I turned to look at my son sitting beside me and noticed his hair was all wet, mud was all over him, and his little blue eyes looked worried about what I was going to say. I burst out laughing, "Oh my goodness what happened to you?" A friend had found a stick to poke the roof of the tent to move the water that had pooled on it. My son thought it would be fun to stand under the gushing water. And the ground was full of mud from the rain and he had been running and playing in it. He smiled back at me in relief that I was not mad. It was hilarious and everyone said that he reminded them of Scott when he was young. Just a young boy having fun in the dirt. Needless to say, I kept his suit unwashed as evidence to show him one day that this story is true.

Once the speeches ended the band started. We ate and visited with everyone. All of a sudden, two vivid rainbows appeared above the vineyard. My daughter pointed and said "My dad did that!" We all felt that this was Scott and his father. They were both showing us a sign that they were with us. It was a moment that we will never forget. There was so much love in the air and I felt supported by everyone. I loved that my kids had their friends and cousins there also. It was very sweet to see the support they had from their peers. I will forever cherish the memories of that day. It was more than everything I had hoped for.

On the flight home from Oregon, I looked at my mom and said that I needed to go to Arizona to look for homes and schools. I had to be out of my home by July 14 and we had nowhere to go in June.

As a mom, finding a school and a community for my children became my number one priority. I focused and prayed so hard for God to guide me. It would be a miracle if my kids got into my school of choice. I knew I wanted a faith-based school because I could not do this alone. I needed God's help and I needed a community. I took a weekend to find both a house and a school. I landed in Phoenix and drove straight to visit a school. Right away I loved the feeling I was receiving. As I walked closer to the front door, I noticed a man coming out and he looked at me.

"Are you my 2 p.m. appointment?" he asked.

"No, but I would love to tour the school!"

"We will call this a God thing and I'll give you a tour since my appointment never showed up."

We walked through the gate and he showed me the classrooms, gym, playground, cafeteria, science room, music room, and art room. I had an immense sense of knowing that my kids would one day attend this school. It felt so right but he then told me that this school had a two- to three-year waiting list. While I was discouraged to hear that, I applied anyway. After a last-minute interview and lots of prayers, just one week before school started I was told that both kids had been accepted. I cried with joy. My prayers had been answered! God placed us in the best educational environment and community for our family. I will forever be grateful for this opportunity.

Our new home miracle happened in much the same way. Being alight with the love and energy of our school miracle, I started looking for a home. I had always dreamed of being in a neighborhood with families with kids running around, within walking distance to my kid's school and parks, near coffee shops and restaurants. During one house tour, I got an instant YES. The home was perfect, with a detached casita for my mom. I put in an offer on the same day and the miracle of our new home happened with the accepted offer. There is so much magic here in my new neighborhood, from the Christmas time celebrations to the families that welcomed us with open arms. Nobody knew our story. It has been a dream come true and I thank God daily for blessing us with this community.

# SECTION 2

# TOOLS FOR
# THE READER

If you feel stuck, there is hope. If you are hiding addictions, there is help. If you are drowning in suicide ideation . . . **you can choose life.**

When Scott died I opted to not cover it up. People were ashamed, alarmed, and quite surprised that I told the truth. If someone asked how Scott passed, I would always tell the truth.

**He died by suicide.**

This upset many. They didn't want me to be so bold and tell the truth, but I refused to lie.

In the two years since Scott's death, I have walked the path of being a widow from my husband's suicide, run a dental practice, experienced grief for me and my children, and dealt with the lawsuit, probate, and family drama.

When I shared my journey on social media, I felt honored that, after just one post, many people connected with me. I realized that in my willingness to share my heartache and struggles, I became a safe person for others to share their own experiences with. I understood how hard it was to find a safe person, so I held their stories with love.

I have had many more people reach out and open their hearts to me. As each individual came to me, they opened up in deep vulnerability and honesty. As they shared, I became aware of how many people were struggling with different kinds of suffering.

There are so many dentists who are currently struggling with their mental health. Many have experienced deep depression and many have attempted suicide. I am also saddened by the number of women who are stuck in abusive relationships. These women are afraid, stuck in the fog of depression and loneliness. Also, a large number of men and women are dealing with deep grief because of loss, addiction, and depression.

My heart felt their pain and I asked God daily how to best help them. I wanted to jump in and save them, but I knew how to be patient and just listen. I now consider them my really good friends and they have taught me so much. They have been a driving force and kept me motivated to write this book. It was in their sharing that I realized my message was important.

Since I listened to a lot of them, I want to share the tools that I have learned throughout my journey and what has helped me find joy even in the darkness.

I believe that each one of these individuals struggle because of the burden of suppression.

**This next section is dedicated to freedom from suppression.**

Freedom occurs when we release the need to suppress.

I am not a therapist. I am not a mental health professional. I am simply a woman who has tasted grief and pain at the most intense levels. I have sought out any and all tools of healing that could help me and my children find peace again.

*I have found glimmers of truth that I believe can help you on your path.*

*I am here for you . . .*

# Chapter 14

# Dentistry

*The lie about dentistry is that it is a wonderful, luxurious-lifestyle career! Many think that dentists make lots of money, work three days a week, and most of all love their career! The truth about dentistry, in my opinion, is that it is a backbreaking career and that you have to hold a lot of fear that comes from your patients.*

The stress that comes from the burdens you carry steals the joy you are seeking. It is my belief that dentistry can be a prison, and that dentists feel stuck. Many dentists love creating the art of dentistry like Scott did, but it is every other aspect of dentistry that is difficult and not often talked about.

When I first started dating Scott in 2006, I remember going to my dentist and he asked me how I was doing and where I was flying to. At the time I was a flight attendant on a private jet and traveling all around the world. I loved my job! I was also excited to share that I had met a wonderful man. I told my dentist all about Scott and I was thrilled to tell him that Scott was a dentist.

As he was looking at my teeth, my dentist's response shocked me. "All dentist's are weird, and did you know that they have the number one suicide rate?"

This was not the happy response that I was hoping for. I could not talk since he was still looking at my teeth. I just lay there with my mouth open as thoughts rushed through my mind. I instantly thought how Scott was different. Scott was not weird, and he was happy! I knew that what my dentist was saying did not pertain to Scott.

*I wonder if this was to prepare me for what was to come.*

A 2021 ADA dentist wellness survey revealed that 54% of all dentists surveyed reported medium or high levels of depression, and 68% of those reporting these levels were age 39 or younger.

Most people don't know this and many don't talk about it.

https://digitaleditions.walsworth.com/publication/?i=758312&article_id=4326411&view=articleBrowser

Dentists have so much on their shoulders. Some have accumulated student loan debt averaging half a million just to become a dentist. Dentists who decide to build their own practice nowadays could potentially go another two to three million dollars in debt to build their practice.

It seems like the rising costs of dental equipment and supplies, coupled with overall inflation, have increased the overall expenses of running a dental office. As a result, to retain their staff, dentists have realized the necessity of providing salary raises to keep up with the increased cost of living. This is particularly crucial because the high demand for dental hygienists and dental assistants has led to a shortage in the workforce. Dental assistants and hygienists know about this shortage and they can name their price. This works to my advantage because I am a dental hygienist, but I also see the other side of dental practice ownership. If dentists don't offer competitive salaries, their staff might be tempted to look for employment elsewhere and accept offers from other dentists, which creates challenges in maintaining a stable and skilled team.

Since I had to run the dental office after my husband passed, I saw and paid all the bills that came through. Dental insurance, especially medicaid, barely covers what the true costs of the treatments are. Many dentists don't like to accept medicaid because of this. It's hard to work for less than you know your value is. The majority of the time dentists are managing insurance claims and facilitating collection from patients. Low collection piles up over the years and becomes unobtainable.

No one prepares you for the reality and stresses of being a dentist. Because of the high equipment costs, the inflation of payroll, and the lack of payment from insurance companies, dentists are required to overproduce to make up for their high overhead. When dentists have to work full time they can start to have physical pain. I know some dentists that have gone through neck or back surgeries. The overworking and pain open the door to the use of pharmaceuticals. Dentists cannot afford to take time off for self-care or vacations so they start numbing the pain to be able to continue working at such an intense rate.

Working as a dental hygienist four to five days a week took a toll on my physical well-being too. I experienced throbbing pain in my neck and lower back, and my wrists showed signs of carpal tunnel syndrome. Recognizing my body's limits, I realized that I could only manage two to three days of work per week without experiencing severe and debilitating pain. Can you imagine the pain dentists who work five to six days a week experience?!

I still can't believe Scott would see 50 patients in a single day! This explains the body pain that plagued him so much.

My life is full of dentists, from the ones I have worked with to the ones I have met at dental conferences and the many whom I call friends. I have heard the majority say that they hate dentistry and that they are over it. They feel stuck and are always calculating their years until retirement. From their perspective, retirement seems to be the only escape. At dental conferences, there is a prevalent culture of heavy drinking that extends well into the early morning hours. I saw that for most dentists, this drinking was a way to combat the suppression that many of them held in their profession. They would use alcohol as the only release against stress. It seemed to be the only way they could numb their pain, quiet their suppression, and have fun.

These truths need to be addressed in dental school to teach dental students how to avoid burnout:

- They need to collaborate with other dentists so they don't have to do it all alone and work five to six days a week.

- Teach them to have mental health awareness for the negativity that is thrown at them daily

- They need physical exercises to keep their core and back strong.

- They need classes on how to manage home life while trying to establish a career.

Dentists should join a dental community that will support their mental health as well as share business wisdom. They need community!

There are too many dentists who commit suicide. This can no longer be brushed under the rug or ignored. Something has to change.

I propose the establishment of a dental helpline where dentists can connect with a fellow dentist or mentor who truly understands the challenges of their profession. Having a dentist on the other line who can empathize with the rigors of dentistry might encourage more dentists to seek support. One possible solution is to involve retired dentists in staffing this helpline. This would not only provide them with a renewed sense of purpose within the dental community but also bring the wisdom and experience they've gained over many years of practice to offer valuable insights and guidance.

I don't know my part in this journey with dentists, but I know I have a part. I cannot stay quiet. We must show up for dentists and support them in the way they need. I have a desire to make a difference for dentists everywhere. If you would like to join me in this cause, scan this QR code

If your drive to go into dentistry is money, you could eventually feel stuck and suppressed. I invite you to find your true passion. Passion and being of service to humanity will carry you further into a fulfilled and happy life.

You are the reason people smile again. You create beautiful smiles and give your patients the confidence they had lost. You are able to hold your patients' fears and gain their trust. You alleviate dental pain that can sometimes be unbearable. You are making a difference in this world—more than you think—and your work needs to shine.

If you are struggling right now as a dentist, you are not alone and you do not need to do this alone! I highly recommend joining a dental partnership organization to take the weight off. Most importantly, learn self-care first. Self-care will allow you to love others better and let them love you. Dentistry is an extremely hard career that those outside this profession cannot relate to. There are ways to lessen the burden and let your heart, instead of your mind, guide you. I know the analytical side will try to talk the heart out of the truth, but let your heart guide you. Being of service with your skills can provide you with so much joy. The more you give back, the more you will see how you truly impact lives.

# Chapter 15

# Mental and
# Psychological Abuse

*The lie is that we can fix someone.*
*The truth is that they have to be willing to make the changes.*

Many who are in abusive relationships suffer the invalidation of their experiences. As I have spoken with many women who are currently being abused, their number one common thread is: They feel crazy. Many are isolated and alone in their experience and the only person they have is their partner—the one who is tangled in and oftentimes the perpetrator of the abuse.

The isolation from friends and family amplifies the abused person's experience in questioning themself and leads them to suppress how they are really feeling. I know that many times when they try to speak up to their partner about their partner's behavior, their partner will soon twist those words (gaslighting) and place blame back on the abused person's own shoulders (blame-shifting).

Oftentimes, when the abused fights for their voice or needs to be heard, they are silenced with punishments. These punishments can be carried out through mean and hurtful words or worse, the silent treatment. The experience of being stonewalled can be one of the most harmful forms of abuse. To be completely ignored and dismissed is a deep wound of neglect and has lasting impacts on a person's well-being and mental health.

Many times when someone is in abuse, they are also dealing with a partner who is most likely stuck in depression, drug addiction, or grief. It all coincides together. When someone is in deep depression they are unable to see or love their partner. When addiction is prevalent, reason doesn't exist. When grief is present, life can lose meaning.

I lived this life with Scott. I know he was not himself toward the end of our time together. The acceleration of his drug use combined with the overwhelming stress from the lawsuit created a toxic environment in our home.

I remember one time when I confronted him about him possibly having an affair, he immediately shut that idea down and stonewalled me for the next few days, which included my birthday. The morning of my birthday I woke up to him still not speaking to me. He did not wish me a happy birthday.

I remember sitting on my porch in an ocean of tears.

Depression doesn't just affect the one who is depressed. It leaks out to those you love.

I had always lived a life of suppression but my interactions with Scott when he was deep in the depths of depression and drug use only exacerbated my need to suppress.

As I have spoken to other women who have similar experiences or worse, they tell me how they feel like they are always walking on eggshells, afraid to even breathe at times.

These women have shared with me their frustration of always questioning, always wondering if they were crazy because their husband would treat everyone else kindly and lovingly but not treat her (the wife) that way.

If you find yourself in the situation I experienced, I want to give you advice I wish I had at the time I was in abuse: Find a local abuse support group to get yourself out of isolation. This will be a safe place to share what you are going through. Many of these groups allow kids to join, or offer Whatsapp chat groups or Zoom meetings. Call a local network on domestic violence and sexual abuse. The national hotline is: https://www.thehotline.org/

Or you can call a local shelter for the abused and ask them to help guide you in creating a plan. You will need a plan to get out and keep you and your kids safe. There are divorce lawyers that specialize in domestic violence. Start documenting; write down events in detail, take pictures, or try to record events. If the police are called, tell them the *whole* truth. I know it is hard to see the possibility of prison for someone you probably still love, but at this point they need professional help and you need safety. Police cannot assume the abuse. They will need a true statement to be able to help you. It can be scary for kids to tell the truth because they don't want their parents to get in trouble. Make them feel safe and educate them in this harsh realization—that their parents need help. Pray with your kids and ask God to help guide you in keeping your family safe and to open doors for you to escape.

Find a counselor. Many now offer zoom calls. Read books about abuse, listen to podcasts on abuse and how some got out. This will help nudge you out of the fog. It is so easy to give up and feel like there is no way out. You are exhausted and don't have the fight in you. Think about your health and how all this turmoil is making you feel: even after sleeping eight hours a night, you still feel exhausted; you are losing your hair; your anxiety is getting worse; you are starting to feel depressed, or worse you have suicidal ideation. Your kids start getting sick all the time; their immune systems are weakened (and so is yours). They are acting out of anger. These are just some signs of a dysregulated nervous system.

# Chapter 16

# Grief

*The lie* about grief is that only some will experience it. *The truth* is that everyone will experience grief. Everyone.

Everyone in their lifetime will deal with grief. It is an emotion of the human experience. Grief can create some of the hardest and darkest times in your life. You will have to completely reinvent yourself because you were so used to having the person you are grieving around you. Experiencing grief involves navigating through various emotions, and often the initial and most challenging stage is anger. The five stages of grief are: denial, anger, bargaining, depression, and acceptance. These illustrate the different emotional phases one will go through while processing loss. Anger is frequently identified as one of the primary emotions in this journey and is considered one of the more difficult aspects to cope with.

You cannot go through this alone. Grief will drown you. So it is imperative to find a grief- or trauma-informed counselor. Find a counselor that can teach you somatic healing like tapping, inner-child work, parts work, Eye Movement Desensitization Reprocessing (EMDR), or one of the many other healing modalities.

Something that will also help tremendously is finding a grief support group in your community, church, school, or online. This is where you will find others are going through what you are going through, or at least something similar to what you are going through. Engaging in a support group eliminates the painful feeling that you are alone. It also allows you to share your story without feeling like a burden to your friends. Though your friends and family can be great to share with, it can sometimes be hard to open up as fully as you need to with them. That is why reaching out for professional help and support groups is essential.

On my journey to process the deep grief of Scott's death, I found the following practices helpful and I hope these can be a guide for you as you process your grief.

**Breathwork**

I found on my journey with grief that breathwork helped me tremendously in processing. I had been struggling with the memory of finding Scott after he had taken his life. This memory haunted me and would arise without warning. I would be walking through the grocery store aisles and the memory would suddenly appear in my mind and I start crying out of nowhere. I remember being at the gym about to start a workout and the memory would show up without notice and I would have to leave immediately because my emotions were uncontrollable.

Through my constant practice with breathwork, I noticed the images began to show up less and less. One during one particular breathwork session, I lay on the ground and the memory and image pulled up stronger than ever before. I felt like I was living that horrific moment once more. Then all of a sudden, I saw that memory and experience being pulled away from me up toward a light. From that moment on I was never again burdened with this memory showing up unannounced. Breathwork has been an extraordinary way to release the stored pain I have held deep within me. I would cry at the end of some sessions and that is just the release that I needed. Breathwork can also be a wonderful tool for releasing anger as well. I have been a part of breathwork sessions in which people would scream, yell, and rage. This is a normal and safe process for releasing anger.

Since breathwork made such an impact in my life I decided to take a breathwork facilitator course and to become certified. I can now provide a safe environment to express stored emotions. Breathwork also allows you to reconnect with yourself. It helps you remember who you are and what your purpose is. It can reunite us with ourselves and bring us back to wholeness.

## Cold Plunge Therapy

Cold plunge therapy is another tool to support you through your grief journey. Cold plunging helps you gain stress resiliency and release what no longer serves you. Each time I would enter into a cold plunge, I was able to release my anger or fear into the water. Then I would pray to God or my angels for guidance or protection while I meditated in the water for three to six minutes.

When I first arrived in Arizona, the first thing I was inspired to do was look for a cold plunge facility. I was lucky enough to find Re|Connect Mind • Body, though I know I was

Divinely guided there. Reconnect starts with breathwork before you go into the cold plunge. While you are in the water, they whisper to you to let go and give the water what no longer serves you. They also will play sound bowls or drums to help facilitate meditation.

I have gone to Reconnect weekly for the past year. My visits there have been a massive contributor to healing through my grief.

## Writing

Writing should be a part of everyone's healing. This is free and can be done from anywhere. If you haven't journaled before, I will guide you. Simply start with a journal and write something every day. If you don't know what to write, start by asking yourself what you are struggling with and one thing you are grateful for at this exact moment. There is always something to be grateful for. Write about *that*.

I remember when my therapist told me to write an angry letter to Scott. She invited me to LET MYSELF be angry that he left us. I had not let myself feel that anger. I was sad. I was heartbroken, but I was also angry. Angry that he chose to leave. Angry that my kids would have to live their lives without their dad. As I wrote this letter, I felt how writing it out released a large amount of pain from within me.

Write. Write. And then write some more.

I highly suggest that you write a book just for yourself, or better yet for everyone to read (like I did). It is all part of releasing the suppression and it speeds up the healing process. I never imagined I'd be writing a book one day. But my wonderful writing coach, Keira Brinton, guided me through the process. Not only did she help with my writing but she also made sure that my nervous system was balanced throughout the process. I did not experience writer's block or burnout. Her expertise was invaluable.

## Dancing

Another amazing thing for relieving grief is to start dancing! I was once told that you store trauma in your hips. Grief lives in the body. It gets stuck in the lungs and is held inside your hips. As you dance, you can move the grief out of the stuck places. Dancing can also be liberating and fun! And that motion of the hips can release some of the stored trauma. Dance is the ultimate release for suppression.

## Exercise, Nutrition, Abstinence

*This is only my point of view and what I experienced when I incorporated this lifestyle. Always consult a health professional for health advice.*

From my personal experience exercise, nutrition, and abstaining from depressants like alcohol was key for me to feel all the waves of grief. I found a gym that has a wonderful community aspect and comradery. I try to mostly eat clean foods to keep my body and mind clear. When I was under a lot of stress I had gut issues. I had acid reflux. I could barely eat anything. My gut could not tolerate food. At one point I could only drink chicken bone broth and eat crackers. I went to see a naturopath to help me repair my gut health. She gave me some supplements and she also mentioned that my gut issues were stress related.

I am a big believer in organic foods, or better yet, foods from a local farmers market. The fresher the better! Once a vegetable or fruit is picked it starts losing its energy and nutritional benefits. Organic *should* have less pesticides but I am aware that it's hard to prove that they do. Fish is my favorite source of protein! Especially Wild Alaska King Salmon! I miss having a freezer full of fresh-caught fish. Will buying organic make your groceries more expensive? ABSOLUTELY!

Years of processed foods, sugar, and large alcohol consumption can make you sick physically and mentally. You will have much more energy throughout your day once you change your eating habits. On the other hand, getting sick will cost you way more than a healthier way of eating. I am all about preventative health so that I can age with a good quality of life!

I look at my 95-year-old grandfather and how he dances the Argentine tango and ballroom three days a week. He walks daily, is a part of a bowling league, and is writing his second book! His first one was about soccer and how it was great for his mental health to have that community and the instruction on proper coaching. He played soccer most of his life. He played on a local team in Quebec City for most of his adult life until he was 80 years old. He eats small meals and eats them slowly. Now, he is writing his autobiography! His life is pretty extraordinary. He was born in Haiti then moved to Quebec City when he was 23 years old. He married a French Canadian woman and they were one of very few interracial families. They faced a lot of racism but that did not stop him climbing the ladder in every field he worked in. His father was a dentist in Haiti and he told me that his dad would accept live chickens, whatever people could provide, in exchange for his services. Many times he would not charge them. His father died of a heart attack at the young age of 52.

Exercise, as we all know, is important for overall health in addition to being a big stress reliever. Whenever I feel anxious, I go for a run or workout and quickly feel much calmer. Running was meditative for me and strength training was my therapy. Now in my 40s, strength training seems to be more important, but I still enjoy running. I love doing two days of lower body exercises, two days of upper body, and a day that incorporates core and dance or yoga. On the weekends, I play outside with my kids and my favorite activity is hiking! There is something about climbing the peak of a mountain that just makes me happy.

If finances do allow for exercising at a gym facility, there are plenty of free workouts on Youtube. If you can afford it and exercise is new to you, I highly recommend hiring a personal trainer. This will keep you accountable, push you harder than you alone would push yourself, and you don't have to wonder which workout to do. Also, you could find a friend who wants to join you in your mission to stay active and stay accountable. Make it fun! You could motivate each other with a deal, like if you don't workout on a day then you owe me $100 or $20. Invest in yourself! It may seem hard at first but soon you will feel the benefits and you will look forward to your workouts.

## Hormonal Evaluation

Depression can often be a symptom from hormone imbalances. Unfortunately, foods, birth control, stress, or too much darkness during the winter season can wreak havoc on your hormones. Get educated on your hormones and all of the changes humans go through in their lifetime. This is also a valuable health care routine for parents to pass onto their children.

## Community

Community: friends, church, gym family, hiking group. Find yourself a healthy community that will have a positive impact on your life. Don't go through grief alone. We are meant to be in community. Find it, let yourself BE in it. Allow yourself to receive. This will be one of your greatest healing agents.

**Be patient with yourself.** *Everyone grieves differently.*

Know that it is okay to be happy and smile. It is okay to have fun. In fact, plan a fun day and play! No guilt! Your true friends will be happy for you. Play will heal you. Laughter will fill you with the joy needed to aid in your healing.

**Trust me, the flight attendants are right.**

**If you are a single parent taking care of grieving children, take care of yourself first.**

This was the best advice that I was given by the organ donor coordinator at the hospital. He was the most caring soul and I had asked him if he knew of any child counselor on the island of Maui. I felt my children needed to talk to a specialist before we traveled back to Alaska. My children had so many questions that I could not answer.

He looked at me with kind eyes as I was signing the paperwork with my hands shaking and my uncontrollable tears falling onto the papers. He was very clear when he spoke these words to me, words that stuck in my mind and guided me as I moved forward on this unknown path. "You will need to find someone for yourself first. Your children will watch you and learn from you on how to heal. You will be their primary healer and it will be imperative for you to seek help."

This message was so powerful that I immediately asked if he could send someone to help me. I was connected with a counselor who guided me through my very first breathwork session. Instantly, I felt my nervous system calm down and I felt God's loving energy surrounding me. During our session I felt this sharp shooting pain stabbing in my heart, and as I breathed consciously I felt peace. This was the first time since the tragedy that I felt a calmness in my heart. It only lasted until our session ended, but I realized how powerful breathing and meditation could be. I met with this counselor three times before we left Maui. This was the beginning of the deep healing journey I would embark on and ultimately lead to the writing of this book. I continued seeking breathwork sessions on Spotify and Youtube.

## Play Therapy

I did find a wonderful child play therapist in Wasilla, for my children. She had a wonderful room with a sand box and two large bookcases, paint, slime, board games, fidgets, and a warm, inviting, atmosphere for kids. She helped them create memory boxes of their dad. Matéas put into his box a snorkeling mask, a fishing lure, and an unwashed t-shirt of Scott's. I was happy that the last memory my kids focused on the most was the day we went snorkeling with friends on

Lanai. That memory included Scott being happy and having fun. I will forever be grateful for this last day with him.

Grief is inevitable. You will either get stuck in it or you will move through it. I have found that as I have used the tools above, I have been able to move through grief and find happiness and joy even after our loss.

# Chapter 17

# Addiction

*The lie* is often that we can drink because everyone does. Or that we can take pharmaceuticals because our doctors prescribe them.
*The truth* is that these will be the numbing agents that might also kill you.

I see it every day: the potential for addiction is all around us. Life is stressful, so you grab a drink or friends take you out to numb out, you drink so heavily that you don't even remember what happened. On my journey, doctors would ask me to give examples of my symptoms. I was always offered a prescription, and I always declined because I knew this was not the answer for me.

It was too easy for my husband to get any prescription from several doctors. He knew all about pharmaceuticals from dental school and truly believed this was the only option. It became a large bandaid to mask the inner pain that created immense inflammation. It is like saying "I'll try one cigarette" and believing you won't get addicted. Pills are addictive agents and they can take over your well-being. If you are depressed and taking antidepressants, drinking alcohol will not help with balancing your mood. It didn't help Scott. He would go into two days of deep depression after a night of drinking, even though he was on an antidepressant. Through watching my husband's lengthy journey with depression, I learned that you have to become your own advocate and educate yourself on the root cause of your ailments. I much prefer to see integrative health doctors or naturopaths. They will dig deep into my experiences and opinions.

We cannot handle our emotions, so we numb them. Maybe we were never taught how to handle emotions from a young age. We were told to stop crying, we were shamed for getting mad, or sometimes we had to hide our own happiness.

# Chapter 18

# Anger

*The lie* *about anger is that it is wrong, it is bad, and you shouldn't feel it.*
*The truth* *is that anger moves you. It is meant to be felt and then it is meant to be released.*

I suffered so much shame in my life for the anger that I felt. Shame is a silent killer that hits directly into your heart. It cripples you and prevents you from releasing and growing. Shame for not using my voice, shame that I shined too bright, shame for my anger, shame for my happiness and smile. I have found that writing about shame has been the most empowering outlet for me to release it. Writing about it, I come back into my power. I had to release this shame to fully own my strengths.

I have done this and because I no longer stuff my shame, hide my shame, or pretend it away . . . I now rise and free myself.

The suppression of my shame created deep anger inside of me. Oftentimes, I would be the most loving mom until something triggered me. I would react in anger with my kids and yell at them over the smallest things. I wouldn't behave this way every day, but when it happened, it scared my kids and me. When I was able to calm myself and reflect upon my actions, I was confused. I did not know why this was happening to me.

Then one day I made the correlation that when I suppressed my anger against Scott and the disconnection we felt, I would be on edge and become impatient and resentful. I was mad at their father for not being present or supportive, and because I had suppressed that anger, it would creep out without my permission onto the people who deserved it the least: my own children.

Each time I acted out in anger, a tsunami of guilt followed. This was not the mother that I wanted to be. I hated this part of me. I felt even more shame because now they had an angry mom on top of an emotionally disconnected dad. I would pray to God to remove my anger and make me a more patient mother. I worked so hard at being a loving and good mother and some days, when I would lose my temper, I felt like I ruined it all.

I apologized to my children and promised them that I would work on my anger because they deserved the best version of me. I would reassure them that it wasn't their fault; it was mine and I admitted to losing control. I didn't want to be the mom who screams at her children with anger.

The darkness was entering me and I never knew when it would show up again. I saw that my daughter could see the darkness in our eyes when anger entered. I started to notice a pattern when it would show up: Each time I was completely exhausted and had suppressed so much anger toward Scott, this pattern would resurface again. I was constantly walking on eggshells to avoid conflict with him. Scott's rage suppressed me, my emotions, and my right to have a voice in the relationship. His fury was scary and I never liked it when he would verbally attack me in front of the children. The anger inside of me would stay suppressed until the pattern would re-emerge once again.

My entire family dealt with anger. We were all in deep levels of pain. Scott was tormented with pain—physical back pain from his work, emotional pain from the lawsuit, mental pain from the stress of running a dental practice, and the pain of disconnection that was a result of drug and alcohol abuse.

I was also in immense pain—the pain of seeing my husband hurt so deeply, the pain of him not seeing or hearing me, the pain of feeling like a single mom while also feeling like I needed to carry my husband's burdens as well.

My children were swimming in pain. Children know. They just do. They know when their parents are in pain. While they are not able to label it, they know the grief. They felt so much pain when the disconnection between Scott and me was prevalent. The children would lash out at each other. Their sibling was an easy target for releasing their inner pain onto.

Realizing that we were all dealing with this anger, I knew that I had to find a solution. I was tired of watching the anger boil up and then erupt like a wild volcano.

## Time-out for Self-Regulation

I soon began walking away when things got to be too much and would take a time-out, taking deep breaths. In these moments I would clear my mind and look within. What was very evident to me was that I was exhausted from doing everything alone and that I so deeply wanted a husband for me and a father for my children. It was time to confront my reality.

That's when I began seeking support. In an effort to move the anger out of my body, I have learned some simple ways to feel instead of suppress. I have found that if I make sure I have **adequate sleep** and take some **quiet time** for *myself* that I am much more able to stay calm and not get tripped into anger. If possible, I aim to **lie down for just 10 minutes** when I feel overwhelmed. It helps me clear my mind and return to being a calm and loving mom.

When I sense a surge of energy and recognize the signs that my emotions are escalating and the volcano within wants to erupt, I close my eyes and take a few deep breaths. Often, I find it necessary to step away from my kids' energies and give myself a moment of stillness. After taking the time for myself, I can come back to my kids and explain calmly, "I started to get overwhelmed and needed some time alone. Please respect that."

Having a conversation with your kids about these strategies beforehand when everyone is calm is key. You can say, "Mom or Dad is learning these new tools and we need to work as a team to respect these boundaries." Realistically, this approach may not work the first time or every time, but you are all **building the new muscle of self-regulation.**

## Tapping

Tapping is another effective tool for calming the nervous system. If you're unfamiliar with the technique, you can find instructional videos online or ask your counselor to demonstrate the techniques for you.

My counselor taught me tapping techniques. She also suggested that I use ice rollers for facial massage on my kids when they start feeling overwhelmed and anger shows up. My kids absolutely love the cold rollers! They love the feel of the cold on their faces and the calming experience it brings.

I know that anger is a part of all of our paths. It is a human emotion. If you struggle with depression, then it is deeper than just an emotion. If you are married to someone who is deep in depression or drug use, then anger is a form of protection. You will need to learn how to let it move through you instead of letting anger move you.

Learning your own triggers and why they happen is an integral part of healing. Write in your journal the incidents and maybe you will start seeing a pattern—an aha moment— as you document the anger arising. Seek nervous system resiliency tools that you can incorporate daily or at least once a week. Talking with a professional to help you see the triggers and the why behind them is invaluable. It will help you understand your kids' triggers as well. Many times I would react because a past experience was triggered. I did not know at the time that I was reacting because I was suppressing my unhappiness and frustration with my husband.

After Scott's death, I noticed my kids would trigger me. They acted toward me like their dad. At first, I perceived this as a threat. The more you carry these negative experiences without processing them, the more the negative experiences clutter your mind. The positive experiences get lost in the clutter and you can't find them. Once you notice that clutter is taking over, you will have to throw away some of that disengagement. You will start pushing trash out. You will need to feel a release and that is when the outbursts happen. I had to learn to not get to that stage and start releasing on a regular basis to avoid arriving at that outburst. Find a way to resolve what is bothering you. Most of the time you will find someone to unload your anger on and usually that is not the one you are mad at.

Be kind to yourself and the ones who love you. Give yourself grace because this practice will take time and work. You will not change overnight. It takes practice and many mistakes along the way. Keep working on it daily and find your own recipe to feel calmer when triggers arise. Find space for you to quiet your mind when you start feeling tired and overwhelmed. Learn ways to avoid conflict and how to resolve it when you can't avoid it. It takes patience and communication skills. Build the skills of emotional intelligence and understand your triggers. Verbalize them with your loved ones and watch when you are tired. Know your limits and don't start a conflict resolution when you are exhausted. Anger is a tool to meet your needs. It is your body giving you some warnings. It is showing you that you need to resolve something.

# Chapter 19

# The Cocktail

*The lie is that fear will protect you, rejection means you aren't good enough, and suppression will hide everything. The truth is that faith will protect you, you are always more than enough, and suppression is only a false sense of security.*

**Fear. Rejection. Suppression.**

This is the cocktail. This is the cocktail that I watched leading Scott into deeper depression, drug use, and disconnect. This was also the cocktail that led to my own personal anger, isolation, and pain.

I believe Scott felt rejection from many people he loved deeply. He created a dialogue that his mother rejected him, and that he was rejected from several friendships that had deep meaning to him. His world was crumbling around him. He felt that if he won the lawsuit, *then* everything would get back to normal. Maybe he believed that he would lose everything if he lost the case. That he would lose me, lose friends, and lose family. He put everything on hold in his life to win this case and he was willing to spend all his money to prove his truth. Seeing this, I was terrified of what would happen if he lost the case. As I saw his mental health declining, I wanted him to let go of the lawsuit and settle. The stress and negativity was all he ever thought about for seven years. There was no room for any positive thoughts. By the end of those seven years, with all the stress, drugs, and alcohol I could not recognize him. Sometimes I wondered if he had bipolar disorder and maybe that is why he didn't want to seek help. Maybe he did not want a diagnosis. Maybe he was afraid if he was diagnosed, he would lose his career, wife, and friends. Or was it just withdrawals from self-medicating? I was left with so many questions about Scott and the inner demons he fought. Sometimes he would say he had the flu, but I knew it was not the flu. It was withdrawals. I was afraid that I was losing my husband and did not know how else to help him.

In my pain, I would see counselors and ask how I could help him. I was unaware that the help he needed was for him to lead his own healing. When I left my counselor, I would return home to Scott and try what the counselor suggested to me. Scott would not go to counseling and he would always tell me that he was in control. He kept pretending he was okay, smiling and making sure to give us enough good days to prove it. He would talk about a beautiful future together: selling the practice, moving to Texas, working only three days a week, and starting to take care of himself. When he would give us the good days, we would bank those to get us through the bad days. When the bad days came, I figured they would pass like they always had.

When I used my voice to tell him to settle the case, I got yelled at and rejected. I would often get the silent treatment for days. Every time he wanted to share more information regarding the case, his energy would be very intense. My body would tense up and my heart rate would rise. I had to tell him that I could no longer sit by him and hear this day after day. It was wreaking havoc on my nervous system. He would not hear my thoughts or advice anyway. I feared for my own health, being around that constant negative energy, and how it was affecting our children as well. They were not able to have an emotionally present father and they could feel his intense anger when he was on the phone discussing the case. At times, he would share his pain with the kids. I never liked that he would involve the kids in his drama. However, I loved the innocence and truth the children had. Sophia would often say, "Why can't both sides just apologize and love each other?" This was simple but true coming from a five-year-old.

My son would not talk about his pain that came from not having a dad to play with him or make him feel loved. He would hide those feelings, and I know now this is why he was so quick to get upset when small issues arose. My daughter noticed how involved her friend's father was. She would cry on my shoulders at night and ask why Dad was not like other dads. This broke my heart. In hopes of getting Scott to play with the kids, I would ask if he could push them on the swings in the backyard. Sometimes he would go and sometimes he would not. I had to *ask* for him to be present, and I could never understand why I had to do that. If he could not come play, I would make excuses to my children and I would try to replace their dad. Inside, I was sad for my kids and I would put on a smile as if everything was okay.

We loved Scott immensely and craved his presence. It truly felt like rejection to my kids when he had no interest in being with them. We felt that we could never be good enough. Maybe we did something wrong? Maybe we should give him more grace and time to rest. He worked hard for our family and was under a tremendous amount of stress with the dental practice and lawsuit. We should just stay quiet and things would get better once the lawsuit was over. This is what I told myself.

He would also tell us that when he won the lawsuit, we would all travel together to Fiji or Africa. He loved jiujitsu and said he would have more time to practice what he enjoyed. He often studied each move and take private lessons when he could. This allowed me to dream ahead for our family, but something didn't feel right. I feared he might not win. What would happen then? How would he handle that? I prayed that we would win even though I wanted to just let it go. I could see a brighter future if we just let go.

Suppression was the container that held back the fear and rejection. It was like a door holding back the flames of the fire. The minute the doors were opened, everything was caught in those flames.

Suppression is like the bandage that has been placed on a large open wound on your body. At first, it might seem like the best option. The blood might stop for a minute, but the bandage will not hold back the heavy bleeding nor will it help the skin heal back together. No, stitches are needed for the deep wounds. Suppression is the source of what didn't work in our lives, the bandage of our emotions. I suppressed my voice by pleasing and trying to make everything "good" while Scott suppressed his pain with addiction.

I believe both of our actions were equally toxic. They created the cocktail that led to a life of disconnect, unhappiness, and deep depression. Fear will hold you captive. Rejection will be the disease that eats away at relationships and steals your joy. Both are fed by the lie of suppression.

## Do not be a prisoner to your fears.

Fears will paralyze you and keep you from growing and will prevent you from reaching your best life.

Rejection will tear apart the love that you have within you and that you have for others.

When I realized that the love and attention I sought were not readily available, I adopted an avoidant and highly independent stance. This independence felt like the freedom I craved, The freedom to be myself without being rejected didn't serve me. While it did create a sense of self-reliance and felt like a shield against potential rejection, it actually closed off my heart and created a deeper disconnection.

I feared that Scott would get worse and that he would lose control over his pain medication. At times, I counted the pills and calculated how many he took per day or week. I feared my marriage was over. I feared leaving. How would he react if I left? My kids love their dad and I'd destroy our family if I left. I felt I had more control in protecting our kids if I stayed because if he had 50/50 custody then I would live in fear the entire week he would have the kids by himself. In reality, our kids were feeling and seeing it all. It was more damaging staying in this toxic environment. Scott probably feared losing me as well.

One time I stood firm and asked for a divorce. I could not do it anymore—the hiding, the lies, the lonely life. I saw how sad my kids were. After my request, he immediately shot up from his chair and professed that I was the only one he ever wanted to be with. He gave me that attention I so needed and went out of his way to be more present, for a while. He said he would quit drinking, and told me he would do anything to keep our marriage intact. He saw that we needed marital counseling and agreed to read books about the topic of marriage. Sadly, the drugs, the lawsuit, alcohol, and suppression from all the pain won over his best intention.

As the case got harder and harder to win, he drank more, took more drugs, isolated more, and consumed himself more with the case.

This led me to become more and more independent. I would get the kids ready for school, drive them to school, drive to work, finish work right in time to pick up the kids from school, make dinner, help the kids with homework, play with them, and get them ready for bed. Again and again, my days were the same—the same lonely world of pain. Since Scott worked most Saturdays, I planned play dates. I took care of any home maintenance repairs. I cared for our chickens, dogs, and greenhouse. I felt like I was independent but that was also what kept me distant and alone. Scott's addictions made me feel more and more reclusive. I could not connect to him anymore. He was not the same man I married and the addictions became his mistresses. They got his full attention and focus.

The cocktail of fear, rejection, and suppression affected both of us in different ways. The effects of these were shown in Scott's addictions and disconnect. The true effects in my life showed themself in my health.

# Chapter 20

# **The Body Speaks**

*__The lie__ is that we are sick because of some strange fate.*
*__The truth__ is, our illnesses are often created from the years of suppression.*

**T**here will be times when your body speaks to you from underneath the trauma that you suppressed.

In September 2020, I received news that my 93-year-old grandmother was ill and had left her home to go to the hospital. She was diagnosed with stage 4 stomach cancer. I was not ready for this news. I always thought she would live to be 100. At the time, I was still messaging her weekly and needed her in my life. I grew up very close with my grandmother and as a young girl, I would often spend the night at her home.

This was happening in the midst of Covid and Canada had shut down their borders. I told Scott that I had to go see my grandmother one last time. At this point, I felt anxiety leaving my kids with their dad for a long period of time. He was not present or emotionally available for them. So I chose to bring them with me. Sophia was six years old and Matéas was four years old. I booked flights to Quebec City and planned to quarantine for two weeks at my dad's house and then I would be allowed to visit my grandmother in the hospital. We were able to enter Canada because I still had my Canadian passport and so did my kids. At the border crossing in Canada, they told me that if I did not quarantine I could go to jail or receive a fine of up to $600,000. I showed them our negative covid test results and entered Canada. I stayed in quarantine until my family told me that my grandma was declining quickly and there was a possibility that I would not have a chance to see her if I kept waiting. I did not want to miss my chance to see her one last time, so I decided to go visit her at the hospital. Yet, I was so afraid. I knew that going to the hospital at this time could mean jail time or huge fines for me, but I knew I could not let my grandma leave this life without me saying goodbye to her. I gathered my children and asked them to not tell anyone we were from the US. I knew this was dangerous. I also knew what needed to be done.

The majority of my family was afraid of us. They were scared of us because we had traveled from America, even though we were taking DAILY covid tests that were showing negative results. I had to ignore everyone's fears, quiet my own thoughts, and follow my intuition.

We drove in silence to the hospital, fear filling all of us. I stopped at McDonald's to pick up my grandma's favorite food: McDonald's chicken nuggets with BBQ sauce. As I sat in the drive through waiting for her order to be filled, a police car pulled up behind me, and fear pulsed through my body. My heart was beating fast and I could feel my breath shorten. Images of me being taken to jail ran through my mind. To my great relief, they were just getting their own lunch!

It was a real journey of faith and overcoming fear to visit my grandma that day. I am forever grateful I did. Not only was I blessed to spend time with her and let her know how much I loved her, but she imparted words of wisdom that day that changed the course of my life.

While we were there with her she loved on my children and told them they could have all of her teddies and dolls from her home! These toys have been such a treasure for my kids and me to remember her kind and loving soul. I smiled as she even wrote a check for $10 to one of the nurses that was taking care of her. The nurse politely declined it but it was proof of the kind of woman she was.

The next day was my 40th birthday, and my aunt offered to watch my kids so that I could visit my grandmother one more time. I was blessed to spend two hours with her all to myself. This was the greatest gift I received on my 40th birthday. It was during this precious time alone with my grandma that she began to share some stories.

She reminisced about me as a little girl when she had to bring me to the airport and send me back to Vancouver. She mentioned how shy I was and that I rarely stood up for myself. It was heartbreaking for her to see me leave and she said it was also very hard for my father. She told me that my father had loved me very much and still did. She shared her own wisdom from when her brother died and how right after he died, she was diagnosed with breast cancer. She said that stress on her body made her sick. She went to a healing facility in Florida and cured her breast cancer.

After she shared this story, she got quiet and told me to be aware of my body. She emphasized how stress can create illness in our bodies. As she spoke these words, something hit me—like truth was coming directly to me, straight from my grandmother's lips. I knew this was a warning that I needed to hear.

Before I knew it, my two hours with her were over. With love and sadness in my heart I gave her a big hug and I kissed her on the cheek. I thanked her for the love she had always given me in my life. I left that hospital room with a nudge that I couldn't ignore: I knew I needed to dive into my own health.

I returned to my aunt's house and was greeted with a beautiful birthday surprise. My children and my aunt had created birthday cards and a little birthday celebration for my 40th. My mother had also sent an order of balloons and cake for me. It filled me with great joy and love to have such wonderful family support. It was the last time I would ever see my grandma and it was the beginning of a new path that I had never imagined.

Once I arrived home in Alaska, the first thing I did was call my doctor and set up a breast MRI. Normally, they don't just give you an MRI by request when you are younger, but my doctor was a breast cancer survivor and she knew the importance of early detection, so she signed off on the request.

Once my MRI results came back, I called into her office immediately. My grandmother's warning and my inner intuition were correct. They had found a cyst and on that same breast my silicone gel implant had a capsular contraction and had ruptured. I could feel this pain and a burning sensation moving through my body. I was scared and started to look for a plastic surgeon to remove the implants and send the cyst for a biopsy. I knew that I did not want to see any of the plastic surgeons in Alaska and I had to find someone highly qualified. I started looking in California, Nevada, and Arizona.

I had a few consults through Zoom before I found a doctor in Arizona that had experience with breast cancer, reconstruction, and breast implant illness. I knew his specialty was the one I could trust.

I had my mother travel with me and the minute we met with my surgeon we knew we had made the right decision. He truly cared for us and reassured us that everything would go well. Not only did he clear my body of the rupture and the cyst, but this was the first time I felt the call to move to Arizona. It was in my recovery that I noticed the peace that I felt being in Arizona. I loved the sunshine and my nervous system felt calm. I had time to reflect on my home life in Alaska. I didn't want to go back to that environment. The months of no sun, the cold, and most of all . . . the darkness that was taking over Scott.

This experience was one of many health scares. Suppression makes the body shut down. In the shutdown, health problems arise. With this new insight my dear grandmother had given me, I started to take a look at my life and the health problems I was dealing with.

The MRI that led to this surgery also propelled me to look at other symptoms within my body: the gut issues that showed up as acid reflux, hoarse voice, thyroid issues, and chronic fatigue. Four months after my breast surgery, I saw another specialist to discover why I had developed a hoarse voice. The ENT did a nasal endoscopy to see clearly down my esophagus and vocal cords. He then noticed that a cyst had formed on my left vocal cord. He asked if I was a singer or motivational speaker because those are the people most susceptible to cysts on their vocal cords. I told him that I was neither and that I worked as a dental hygienist. He explained that I would need surgery to remove the cyst and that during my recovery I could not use my voice for three weeks. I wondered how it would be possible to not use my voice, with my son being four and my daughter six at the time. Who would take care of me and how would I communicate with my children? At this time, Scott was not helping with the children or me.

I was fortunate that the timing of my surgery happened when Scott's father and his father's wife came to visit for our niece's high school graduation. His father and his father's wife were able to help with the kids and me. I used a white board to write things down or used my phone's voice activator for a word or sentence to communicate with my son, who could not fully read yet.

My symptoms were shining a light on my inner turmoil. My years of suppression had created havoc in my body. I knew this was a true result of suppressing the truth within me my whole life. My physical symptoms were mirroring my emotional suppression. My mother also claimed that she thought this was God telling me to use my voice because I was repressing and not speaking my mind.

My body had started sending out signals when I was in my mid-30s. I was living in a toxic environment. I went through several health scares that caught my attention. That is when I knew that I had to make some changes. Even though I saw many doctors, none said the root cause was STRESS. I now know this as the truth: my body was reacting to my environment and showing up as chronic illnesses.

My body was demanding a change. One of my favorite quotes by Gabor Maté is "If you don't say 'no,' your body will say it for you through symptoms and chronic illness."[3]

I didn't know how to say no. I was never taught how. I didn't understand how to speak my truth. Instead, I suppressed and in the suppression my body was speaking up for me.

I am grateful that after the second surgery to remove the cyst on my vocal cords I woke up and made changes. This is when I began to let my voice be heard more. I started to release the emotions that had been stuffed down with the years of suppression.

If your body had a voice, what would it tell you? Have you taken notice of the correlation of your body's illnesses to your suppressed emotions?

Start writing notes about what you notice on certain days about your health. Do you feel fatigued even though you slept eight hours? Or do you just feel fatigued all the time? How does your gut feel? Do you have acid reflux? Write it all down. Start noticing patterns from month to month. Are you losing

---

[3] Gabor Maté, *When the Body Says No: Exploring the Stress-Disease Connection*, (Hoboken: John Wiley & Sons, 2003).

your hair or are you having premature graying? I am not a doctor, but these are my personal experiences and what I noticed in my body. Are you noticing new hip strains, knee pain, or lower back pain? My body was starting to speak very loudly. I felt like I was crazy and like I was a hypochondriac. People looked at me and thought I looked healthy. I am fit and I ate well. I didn't FEEL well though. Create space to truly listen to your body. Notice these slight changes and do not ignore them. Managing your stress and nervous system is crucial to avoiding chronic illness and pain. We will all go through stress and grief in our lives and learning tools to release those energies can be life saving.

Your body holds deep wisdom.

You will be guided so trust your inner knowing or gut instinct.

# Chapter 21

# Apologizing
# Keeps Us Safe

*The lie is that if we apologize, we will be safe.*
*The truth is every apology that isn't real keeps us in the cycle.*

When a truth needs to be spoken and we fear it can't be received, one way we suppress it is by apologizing. That can come from saying sorry, but it can also come in the form of playing small.

This cycle of apologizing or playing small is created by suppression. Growing up, I was extremely shy and I always wanted to be the "good girl" as defined by my family. My need to be loved by all kept me apologizing and over pleasing. I didn't have any boundaries for myself. I didn't know how to have them. I was never taught.

I remember in fourth grade how this bully kept putting everyone down. He was always mocking a poor little girl that had Down syndrome. He used to criticize my appearance, labeling me as ugly and mocking my frizzy hair. Additionally, he would belittle me by calling me stupid, especially when I had to attend a separate reading group because of my language barrier. The process of transitioning from French to a new language, English, was already challenging, making his comments even more hurtful. I saw him bully many people in my class and nobody ever stood up to him, not even the teachers. During a music class, he humiliated me and that day, I reached a breaking point. On impulse, I grabbed my flute and struck him in response.

Fed up with his constant assault on my self-esteem, I decided to take a stand. In my attempt to be the first one to confront him, I ended up in the principal's office. The bullying persisted until we eventually went to different high schools. Standing up for myself got ME in trouble. I wasn't protected; I was given a consequence. This began the pattern of suppressing for me. I learned then that speaking up for myself would ultimately end in my own pain. It seemed better to stay quiet and endure than speak and get in trouble. Because I was taught that the only form of speaking up was physical retribution, I equated speaking up for myself with punishment. Had I known HOW to speak up in a way that would have protected me, things might have been different. Seeing that the teachers and administrators didn't set boundaries for this bully, how could they teach me something they themselves did not know how to do?

We apologize because if we do speak our truth, we get hurt. I can now look back and see how this cycle happened over and over throughout my life. Once my dad remarried, I was not treated kindly by my stepmother. She was jealous that my dad would get so happy to see me and spend time with me. I never told my dad how she treated me while he was at work. I didn't want to cause any conflict. He was in love and happy. I didn't want to change that for him. My stepmother's sister lived next door with her children. When I left for a few days to stay with my grandmother, I would leave my big suitcase at my dad's house and just pack what I needed. Once when I returned to my dad's house, I noticed that some of my clothes were missing. I didn't want to point fingers but I had a really good idea who might have taken them. I told my dad and I got all of my clothes back, but I also got bullied by these girls for telling. Once again I used my voice and it came back to hurt me. I wasn't being protected by those who were supposed to do so.

It seemed that things would get worse if I spoke my truth. I now see that a lot of these experiences were my own fault for not setting boundaries, but suppressing was also a way to protect myself. I was allowing people to treat me with no respect. I was afraid of conflict and even to this day, I get nervous when I have to speak up for myself or my children. I prefer to please others to keep the peace. My children are the opposite of how I was as a child. They are not shy and they are confident. They get in trouble for speaking their truth. I now have to stand up for them and I know that it may harm my own relationships with other parents but I will always stand up for my children. I cannot perpetuate the cycle, even though it is more comfortable for me to stay in it. I have decided to break this cycle by speaking my truth.

I can now see how suppressing my voice kept Scott and me in a toxic cycle. I was wired from a young age to not speak my truth. I was taught from every experience when I got in trouble for using my voice that it was safer for me to be quiet and appease.

I see how this has played out in most areas of my life, the need to please and stay quiet. This was the root of suppression for me. I always wanted to be good, follow the rules, not speak my truth unless it was nice. This was the rhythm of suppression that I had always lived.

I found that I was always apologizing when it wasn't necessary, whether for myself or my kids, keeping me trapped in a cycle. Now that I have decided to break free, I am actively learning about boundaries and expressing my truth.

I learned that while standing up for ourselves and our family might result in losing some friends, I'm instilling in myself and my children the importance of not tolerating bullying behavior in the future.

I bought books for myself and my children to help us learn how to set boundaries. My counselor and I worked together to help me find confidence using my voice. When something doesn't feel right with someone or I feel wronged, I now communicate with that person in a calm, peaceful, and firm manner. My message is clear and I stand strong in my boundaries. This does not come easily for me, as I like to avoid conflict at all cost. I'd rather stay quiet and keep those emotions inside. However, I know too well that it ends up hurting my nervous system and immune system.

I teach my children to communicate to their peers in that same calm, peaceful, firm manner if they feel hurt and wronged. Learning to communicate properly can help alleviate conflict and set those boundaries early on in relationships.

I did find that since speaking my truth was new to me, many were caught off guard when I used my voice. They said things like "you've changed" or "that doesn't sound like you." They were right! I was changing, growing, and learning to set boundaries! I got a lot of push back and I had to be okay with that. I don't like hurting people's feelings but setting limits is not hurting anyone. People may feel hurt by your boundaries, but boundaries help with communication and behavior between people.

I see this working already with my kids. When one of my kids is bothered by a friend making fun of them or calling them names, I tell my child to go up to that person calmly and tell the person that it hurts their feelings and that they would like them to stop doing that. Most times this does not stop the behavior right away. Setting the boundary has to be repeated several times, but after my child has repeated their boundary two or three times, I also tell my child to tell the friend that they will lose them as a friend if the unkindness continues. Now, my child would have to follow through.

I am talking about my child's peers who keep putting my child down and do not want the best for them. It is important to me that my children learn to seek the right circle of friends—the ones that will lift them up, encourage them, love them, and be a listening ear. No jealousy. Not a revengeful or negative friend. It is important to start noticing those characteristics at a young age. Who are your authentic friends? Who will gossip about you behind your back? Who will stand up for you? Who will be there when you are sad? Who will be there when you are shining bright and succeeding. Do they have the same values as you?

One step I took toward speaking my truth was writing. I wrote letters to someone in my journal. Or I would practice with my counselor. It gave me confidence. I would get very nervous and still do when I feel that I need to address something. My speaking up is not perfect. I will continue to learn along the way and I will no doubt make many mistakes.

# Chapter 22

# Living in Cycles and the Deadend

*The lie* is that what is familiar is always safe.
*The truth* is that sometimes what is familiar is toxic for us.

Cycles and patterns are what keep us stuck in our comfort zone. It keeps us going back to what is familiar, even if it is not a healthy environment. Life gets hard, and so, in the hard moments we seek out help. The second the darkness leaves, it is easy to fall back into the cycle of the old and comfortable: the numbing, the stuffing, the ignoring. Somehow in that cycle we forget. We forget how much we need help. We forget about the pain, and we think that in the suppression, we are okay.

This is the cycle I lived in over and over. I lived in it each time things would get really hard in my marriage. I watched myself come to the edge and do what needed to be done to change our environment, then things seemed to get better for a time. After a while I would slip back and the quieting of my truth would occur, which was only the onset of the next cycle.

I saw this cycle with Scott. Things got really dark for him, and so he would start diving into more prescription pills, drinking . . . anything to numb his heavy pain. Once he was numbed, it seemed for a minute that the pain wasn't there. So we all felt we could somehow keep moving forward. But it was really only the start button to the cycle being pushed. The cycle would run its course over and over again.

The cycle creates a level of insanity.

This cycle is bred from the silence of suppression.

I remember a time when we wanted to go camping for two days at a lake 45 minutes from our home. This campground was first come, first served for camp spots. I agreed to pack the RV and head there earlier with the kids to set up camp. Scott would meet us there after work to enjoy a family weekend. We loved camping and it was a great way to get away from the norm at home.

My kids were only four and six years old. They got out of the RV and started playing with their toys outside while I arranged our campsite. We were all excited to see Dad once he got off work and we had planned to head out on the lake with our little inflatable raft. We would go fishing with Dad. This was Scott's favorite thing and the kids and I thought this would be great for him to do after work.

"Dad's here!" the kids yelled when they saw his truck driving toward our campsite. He got out and they ran to give him great big hugs. He lifted them up in his arms and that melted my heart. Seeing Scott love the kids always made me happy. This felt like a loving family, my dream of a united family.

Scott then walked in the RV, went to the bed, and lay there with his phone. I sat outside with the kids and played with them. I asked if he was hungry and he said no. I fed the kids and thought that I should give Scott some down time after work. A few hours passed and I walked into the RV and asked if we could go fishing on the raft as a family. He said no and that he was tired. I was disappointed and thought to myself, why did we come here then? Will I be by myself again to take care of the kids and entertain them? We all know that kids that age need constant attention and someone needs to always be with them. That someone was me. Always. I was grateful for that, of course, because I love my children and I know how fast these precious moments go each year. However, I wanted to enjoy these moments *as a family.*

I packed our little raft to head out and I saw Sophia going into the RV. She went in to ask Dad if he could please join us. If anyone could get him to come it would surely be his adorable children. However, this was not the case. He got out of the RV, walked to his truck, got in, and drove off.

In an instant, my stomach tightened. My kids ran to me crying and I held them tight. I felt a mix of sadness and anger. How could he do this to his children? They were asking why Dad left. They thought it was their fault, that they were bad. I tried to call him but I got no answer. The fun family camping weekend was over. I did not want to stay there by myself. I just wanted to go home.

With the kids crying, I started packing. They wanted to go home too and see their dad. I realized how this was so damaging to our kids. They did not understand at all why Dad would do that. I was not sure what to do next. I drove the RV home. I put on a movie for the kids once we got home so that I could talk to Scott. I was very worried for him and asked him if he had suicidal thoughts. I told him that his behavior was concerning and that it affected all of us. He said that he did not have suicidal thoughts and that he was just sad about his father. His father had been diagnosed with cancer and Scott was very close to him. He said that he would be okay and that he just needed rest. I asked if he would be willing to seek professional help and he declined. "I'll be fine" or "I'm okay" was always the answer. I asked him to stop drinking while he was taking the pharmaceuticals. He said okay and things got better for a while. He stopped drinking for a month. He seemed happier and that drew me back into the cycle.

I went through a cycle of *I'm done with this marriage* and *I'm never leaving*. I went to counseling and asked how I could best help my husband. I was told to give him empathy and compassion. I did that, but sometimes I would get frustrated because I didn't understand. I didn't understand everything that he was going through. It was hard to give empathy to someone who was so distant to his own kids. If I did not understand, my kids definitely did not.

I would get upset when he was constantly on his phone. I would speak up but that never seemed to help him want to be present with his kids. He would yell and then we would get the silent treatment for days. Then I would think about leaving again but those logistics seemed impossible. Where could I find a safe apartment to live in, in Wasilla? The rent was very expensive and I'd have to work five days a week. I would have to hire someone to take the kids to school and pick them up. Who would take care of my kids when Scott would have the kids? He could barely take care of himself.

Then one day, he would come back from work and sit in the living room playing his guitar and the kids would sing and dance. That made me so happy. We would talk and pretend nothing had ever happened. He would give me a big hug and say, "I love you." He would often say, "You are the only woman I ever want to be with." I felt loved and his hugs made me feel safe. I loved him too and I held on tightly to the Scott I knew well. I knew his beautiful heart and what we hoped for as a family. We wanted to grow old together and felt very happy to have two wonderful children. There was always hope. I loved how some of my friend's husbands were friends with Scott. They loved him and they always had a great time when they were with him.

Knowing the cycle so well, your grief and fear come swarming in. I would think about marriages that made it through affairs, addiction, and depression. We could make it through too, but it all seemed to be on my shoulders. So I continued doing all the work so we could make it through. I felt overwhelmed raising my kids on my own, helping my husband emotionally, and managing my own well-being. Some days were quite overwhelming. These cycles are similar to a whirlpool that we often get stuck in. When you are there, you know. I see you and I know. There is hope for you to get out of this whirlpool. What I learned is that I had to start taking care of my mental and physical health.

# Chapter 23

# Unfulfilled

*The lie is that we need more things.*
*The truth is we need more stillness and space to look within.*

I believe one of the greatest illusions that we struggle with every single day is wanting more stuff. More money, more toys, more vacations . . . MORE.MORE.MORE! I have seen this many different times in my life. I have watched people I didn't know and some people I love seeking to find fulfillment in the "things" but always left feeling super unfulfilled and unhappy.

When I was 20 years old I became a flight attendant. After 3 years of working for Air Canada, I was offered an amazing opportunity to fly as a private-jet flight attendant. I loved my job. The best part was that I got to work with my best friend. We traveled the world and I got to have extraordinary experiences. The people I met and talked to changed my life. I was lucky enough to fly with a former United States president, other political superstars, and some of the greatest musicians and pop artists in the world. I found that while some celebrities were snobby and rude, most were actually very kind to me, even though I was just their flight attendant.

With these individuals it seemed that there was no separation between their wealth and titles and me. I will always remember how they made me feel. It was a lesson of being a kind human, no matter who you are.

I also witnessed something profound.

I was taught by society to believe that if you were famous, life was perfect and amazing but I saw firsthand that it was not. I remember seeing and feeling the deep unhappiness that lived in the midst of all their wealth. These celebrities were living most people's dreams! They owned a private jet and were able to fly anywhere they wanted to! Most people would think that this is pure happiness!

**I found this was not true.**

Many of these celebrities were extremely unhappy. Their lives were filled with everything you can imagine, but it was a life that was extremely UNFULFILLED.

The continuous SEEKING for more made them feel DEPRIVED.

I saw this happen with Scott.

Scott could not let go of the lawsuit. He had to prove he was right and he wanted to keep his money. It destroyed his joy, his experience of life for over seven years. The truth is that he lost more money trying to win the lawsuit. He had remortgaged the house and taken out loans to pay lawyers and he worked six days a week. He never wanted to downsize, though I had requested we do so. I said that I wanted my husband back and I would rather have him with less stress.

Bills and the lawsuit seemed to be the biggest stressors for him. Downsizing and letting go of the lawsuit was my solution. He would agree to neither. Why? Probably because our home and his practice are what he worked for. That was HIS VISION, HIS TRUTH. The big house, the large dental practice . . . maybe for him those things defined his worthiness. Losing those things would make him feel weak, while to me letting it all go felt like freedom and happiness.

I know Scott was not alone in this: drowning in debt and dealing with litigation while aching for the grander lifestyle.

I have met women who have told me the stories of their husband, brother, or friend who died by suicide because they were up to their ears in debt, or their business was crashing.

When we seek outside of ourselves to feel fulfilled, we put ourselves in a very precarious situation. Outside situations can always change. So if we are putting our worth in our bank accounts, our businesses, or how many cars and toys we have, then we become fickle. When we are seeking to be fulfilled by these *things*, we can also be left empty. This chapter is a reminder to stop putting your worth in the outside world. Stop believing that you will finally be happy if you have a certain amount of money in the bank, your company hits a certain revenue number, or you get to drive your dream car.

I watched my husband lose his life years before he actually died. He lost the essence of living when he focused on winning the lawsuit. He lost his joy when he focused on making more and more money.

**We will never be fulfilled by the outside; this is only an illusion that shows up again and again, playing tricks on us with material things.**

You may reach your goal but at what cost? Check in and ask yourself, "How is my marriage, my health, and my relationship with my kids? How is my connection with God?" Let this be the gauge with which you measure your fulfillment level.

To feel fulfilled in life you first have to love yourself and learn who you truly are. What is your purpose in life? If your purpose is money, you will give money power over your life. If your purpose is love and being of service to others, you will be fulfilled. Using creative energy to bring light to the world will bring you joy. Money will come and go and if you give it power it will destroy you when your bank account is low. If you truly believe in your mission and your calling, then use that fire inside to propel you forward. Money will come back when you are following your true calling and purpose.

Chapter 24

# Divisiveness

*The lie is that we are superior over other cultures, religions, beliefs, and political views.*
*The truth is we are not superior or inferior. We are one.*

**Division is the corruption of humanity.**

This is what I believe creates so much havoc in our lives, families, and communities.

I cherished a book that beautifully united two religions: *The Book of Joy* by His Holiness the Dalai Lama and Desmond Tutu. It serves as a wonderful example of the shift our world needs by embracing diversity and fostering compassion for others.

We experience division in ideas, religions, and governments.

From my own research and perception I have found that faith is the number one factor that comes into play to heal people from darkness. Divine intervention comes in for many whom I have spoken to. This divine source of light provides hope, guidance, community, prayer, and kindness but many will not speak on this topic. They don't want to step on toes or rock the boat.

*My gut tells me to elaborate on the subject of faith.*

I cannot talk about suicide, depression, and abuse without bringing in the concept of faith in a higher power. I know that you might have triggers with the word God. For many, it is because of their religious trauma.

The problem is, many people associate God with religion. Religion DIVIDES. I've seen people being divided by religion everywhere. In my travels around the world to places like Bali, India, Pakistan, Hong Kong, and Dubai, I noticed something simple: God is God, no matter your religion.

God is love and God wants us to love everyone, with no judgment or fear. God placed diversity in humans for a reason: for us to learn from each other and realize that we are all one. The purpose of our diversity is to help us connect to the DIVINE.

Each religion has positive aspects like creating hope, community, and instilling good behavior toward each other. Why not build a bridge of union from religions, instead of a brick wall? It's confusing to me why we judge people based on their religious beliefs. Everyone is on their own life journey, and most seem to believe in a higher power. What if we all united together and collaborated with our own unique gifts and wisdom?

In both my family and Scott's, there are various beliefs, but I've noticed one shared commonality: Jesus guides us through God's light and following His teachings brings us closer to

God. Reading books about other religions has contributed to my spiritual growth. However, I've noticed that religion can create separation. When we identify with a specific religion, like saying "I'm a Christian," "I'm Jewish," or "I'm a Scientologist," people often categorize and judge us instantly.

What if we simply say, "I believe in a guiding Source and we are all connected"? Religion has the potential to lead you away from God, but God is love. Seeking Him will reveal His guidance. It's crucial to rely on His understanding rather than our own. I am submitting to Him, trusting Him wholeheartedly—an acquiescence to the Lord. Our purpose is to serve one another with love. Some parts of the Bible may be misinterpreted by humans. Don't let their misinterpretation persuade you to not read the Bible. Seek God on your own. Find God. This is how I believe you will get OUT of the dark.

Do I aspire to be the spokesperson for this topic? No, I'd prefer to remain silent and focus on my family. However, I feel a calling from God to bring attention to this issue because our world requires a positive change. I believe that by working together, we can promote kindness and offer prayers for one another. It's essential to elevate the vibrations on earth and eliminate limiting beliefs. Let's begin by understanding what Jesus actually taught, rather than the fear-based interpretations that many people may have taught.

The experience of the Covid pandemic highlighted how people can instill fear, causing widespread distress and division. Your inner knowing (God) may have questioned the sense in this. Watching the news could escalate anxiety. Perhaps, trusting in God rather than relying solely on the news might have brought more ease during that time. Covid became an unfortunate example of division among humans, leading to the loss of friendships over vaccination choices. The question arises: Why do we need to be so divided? More love and compassion could significantly reduce destruction and hate.

Help me raise the vibrations on this planet. Do it for the world, but first do it for YOU.

Start today and communicate with God. Begin by establishing a connection with God, or whatever term resonates with you if you're uncomfortable using the word "God." I went through a decade that I couldn't use that word either because I felt conflicted by some church teachings that seemed fear-based. Now, I realize that certain teachings are man-made and meant to instill fear. However, I hold belief in Jesus and His teachings.

Consider reading the Bible or a Bible app. If something doesn't align with your feelings as you read, feel free to let it go. There's a wealth of goodness and wisdom in there. I advocate for a global day of prayer, which is what *should* make the news, encouraging people to pray for their country and our planet. We need to pray for leaders with the courage to unite us, reveal truths about the pharmaceutical and food industries, and lead a collective shift to save our planet.

Let's take inspiration from how native cultures respected nature and imparted wisdom. The earth and future generations are at stake, and many people carry uncertainty and divisiveness in their hearts. We must trust and explore God's teachings to guide us through these challenges. Words have the power to heal the broken hearts of the world. If we release our selfish interests, our minds can be enlightened and we can be connected!

It is crucial for top leaders, the news, and all other media to collaborate and share God's words, unveiling the truth for selfless reasons. Imagine if pharmaceutical companies were honest about their products, which could potentially save millions of lives and prevent family hardships.

There is a collective yearning for truth, which can be found in God's words. It's essential to make a habit of reading them daily, steering clear of the news that is only filled with darkness. Be cautious about what you watch, listen to, and absorb—it shapes your thoughts and enters your heart.

As more people rise up to share Jesus's light, we can defy the fate of our planet. Following God's law will contribute to a positive outcome, while neglecting His law leads to destruction and increases darkness. Overcoming divisiveness requires embracing Christ's love and truth.

Scott chose no faith, which I never judged. He often mocked several religions. He was very smart and liked facts. Religion scared him. Once we had kids, I decided to go back to church. I knew how it impacted my life to have that foundation. I found a wonderful Christian church in Wasilla. I loved how pastors shared the Bible with real life stories. I loved the music and singing.

When I started going back to a church community and deepening my faith, I experienced a wave of sadness and wanted to cry. I felt sad because I had missed this community of faith. It was so beautiful. It was important for me to bring my kids to church. Most of my friends were going to church too and brought their kids as well. I did love that Scott never said that I could not go. We often asked him to join us. I explained to him how church was not what it used to be. I even asked him to play the guitar at church, but he always declined.

Unfortunately, sometimes I would feel guilty going to church because it was Scott's only day off and we wanted to spend time with him too. I was torn. I loved my church and how I felt when I returned home from church. It was a community for me. It shined light on my life and thoughts. I would pray with the kids at home. Scott seemed to love that for them. I am grateful that he did not speak against it in front of the kids.

I know that when I prayed for him at the hospital, he could see it was all true. The doctors had told me that he was completely brain dead but I know his spirit was in the room. He was being kept alive with so many machines. He shed a tear while I prayed for him. I will never forget that moment. I know in my heart that he finally believed and saw Jesus that day. I stayed for hours by his bedside at the hospital, telling him that I forgave him, that I will forever be grateful for him, and that I loved him and always would. Most of all I begged him to protect our beautiful children.

Darkness: the heavy blanket that weighs down on many of us. It was the sinking hole that Scott couldn't escape from. It was seeping into every corner of our lives: our business, our home, and our family. I could feel and see this darkness in his eyes.

As I started to speak my truth, I had many tell me about their close calls with suicide and I always ask the same question:

"What made you decide to live that day?" Some said that something inside their heart (God) said to stop and go ask for help. They would grab their phone and call the suicide helpline or a friend, or go tell their significant other. They used their own voices to ask for help and spoke their truth about suicidal thoughts. Some shared that there was a divine intervention that did not allow them to die. All of them that have shared with me their stories now believe in GOD! It is extremely important for you to see this and the reality that without faith and belief in God, there is no hope.

Scott did not believe in God or have any spiritual beliefs. He was very much all about tangible facts. He did not grow up with faith and he was not open to it as an adult. This is why I believe it is crucial to plant those seeds in ourselves at a young age.

I witnessed darkness for many years and how it tries to keep us away from God. It was such a strong darkness that, at times, I could not lie down near my husband. I was afraid of him and God was protecting me.

We need more love, kindness, compassion, and empathy around the world.

# Chapter 25

# Moving away
# from the Light

*The lie is that when the darkness is upon us, there is no way out. There is an illusion that when the darkness hits, you have no choice. But this is a lie.*
*The truth is that there is always hope.*

Moving away from God and His light will only bring you to the darkness. It's not evil or demons that bring you to the darkness, but just moving away from God that does. The thought of demons or evil creates fear. Fear creates anxiety and sleepless nights. I did feel Scott's darkness because he kept moving further away from God. His choices brought on more darkness and feelings of guilt, shame, and anger.

I believe that we can emerge from darkness transformed. We accrue the wisdom that will unite our body and soul. Your connection to God deepens and you have a profound capacity to love all things. You become more authentic as you heal. The process of healing is there for a lifetime. I am seeking growth and light every day. It brings me joy and excitement.

There is an indefinite wealth of knowledge and there are many wonderful writers, speakers, and healers in this world. When we are suffering, it is very hard to see WHY? Why is this happening to me? Why would God allow such horrific events? They are lessons that we come on earth to learn and feel from.

I felt that I had no choice but to focus on the NOW for my family once Scott passed. I did not feel guilt because I knew how much love we had given him. I also knew that this decision was completely up to him. He chose not to ask for help and be completely honest about his thoughts and inner turmoil. My children needed me the most right then and I had to make extremely hard decisions. My deep devotion to God and his guidance was crucial. I knew to avoid alcohol and allow space to truly listen to my inner guidance. Courage, strength, and using my voice was my new commitment.

With the lawsuit, both sides felt betrayed and hurt. However, the way they decided to handle the situation created more conflict and ended up having a ripple effect on everyone around them: the kids, the family, friends, and staff members. That negative energy was extremely toxic.

Sometimes just a slight shift in perspective can change your entire outlook on a situation. For example, on day two of my writing adventure in Mill Valley, California, with my writing coach, Keira Brinton, the power went out at 10:30 p.m. and was still out when we woke up at 5:30 a.m. We had a busy morning planned, filled with a mastermind meeting and writing. And our computers and phone batteries were at only 20%. After our morning prayer routine, I said, "Why don't we go to a coffee shop to work?" What we could have done was stay home, lying in bed and doing nothing while hoping the power would return in time for our meetings. We were in the treehouse and it was cold, but we got ready in the dark and left.

We found a wonderful coffee shop 10 minutes away and we were able to start working by 7 a.m. We had light, electricity, and the best coffee. It thought about how many people were in the dark and saw no way out . . . but there is always a way out.

There was a time when I moved to Arizona that I wanted to shut down all of my social media accounts and hide. I needed a break from the world. I did not trust anyone anymore.

One day, my mother told me that everyone was wondering how we were doing. I made a post on Facebook to show that we were doing okay. I had a huge response showing that people cared and loved hearing from us. That felt good and I viewed this as a way to touch base with the masses. I did not have time to be on the phone calling everyone to keep them informed.

If I had never started posting my story and sharing, I would have never heard from those that messaged me and shared their stories. For some, I was the first person that they trusted to tell their truth to. It was their first release and it made me realize that it was important to keep sharing to encourage others to look within.

I was shown how many people are in abusive relationships, deep grief, depression, addiction, chronic pain, or diagnosed with illnesses. Not a single one of them could see a way out, but I am here today to prove to you that there is always a way out.

It starts with planting a seed of hope, and you can do that by starting a conversation with God. Your faith is the first seed of hope. Start by asking for guidance and protection. Give Him your fears with a grateful heart. Thank Him for one thing in your life. It can be as simple as thanking Him for your breathing.

God can create miracles.

Continue this practice every day, communicating with God, the Source, the Higher Power, your heart. I have seen this work in my life. Miracle after miracle, doors kept opening and it amazed me every time. I prayed to protect my children and to shower them with love. I asked that He make His presence known in their hearts. I knew I could not do this alone. I needed God to help me give love and hope to my children.

When we flew home from Maui many friends asked what we needed. I didn't know what we needed. Being in shock, I couldn't think straight and I did not know HOW to ask for help. I had become the most independent woman and never asked for help. This was not a muscle that I had used in decades.

You know what happened? MIRACLES!

- God gave me the chance to revive Scott.

- God then organized an army of angels to take care of Sophia, Matéas, and myself.

- Angels appeared in the form of friends.

  - friends who took care of my children while I went to the hospital

- the friend who drove me to the hospital and back while I was in complete shock
- friends who booked our tickets home
- friends who picked us up at the airport and even brought our dog to the airport
- friends waiting for us at our home when we arrived
- friends sending us meals every day for three months
- friends and family members sending us money when we didn't have any

- Scott shed a tear while I prayed for him at the hospital.

- The organ donor specialist guided me to take care of me first.

- My counselors gave me guidance and tools.

- The two rainbows appeared at Scott's celebration of life.

- My mom was finally approved for her green card after four years and moved to Arizona to help take care of my children and me.

- The staff at the office continued working so that the business kept running, taking that problem off my shoulders.

- The offer on my house "As is" prevented me from having to stage it for the sale.

- I found the best school for my children and they were accepted.

- I found the right home for the children, my mom, and me.

- I found the right people to encourage me to write my book.

- Friends wrote individual prayers and created a prayer book when I left for my writing adventure.

Now, all of this right here was God showing up for us and sending all of our friends in action. I sought God and He paved a path forward, one day at a time.

Our friends started a GoFund me, because I had to keep paying the bills and I had no access to funds. There was a cooler placed at the end of our driveway and people would drop off baked goods and meals for us, for three months. My kids would get so excited every day to see what we would get for meals and baked goods. This brought them joy. Friends from afar also found a local chef to prepare meals for us for a week at a time, or they would pick days to Doordash food for us.

I would sit daily in our calming center with each child, and sometimes several times a day. I noticed over time my children would choose a positive feeling card like joy. I would ask them what made them feel joy. They said that they felt joy when people sent meals, baskets of activities, stuffed animals, beautiful messages, and donations to pay our bills. They would often ask me, "What are we going to do now without Dad?" But many people cared for our family and that was giving my children hope that we would be taken care of without their dad.

# Chapter 26

# Don't Do it Alone

*The lie* is that you are a burden to others when you ask for help or share your difficulties.
*The truth* is that people are eager to help and it brings them joy to be of service to others in need.

I feel that those who struggle the most with the darkness of suicide are the brightest people. These that the darkness tries to drown are the ones with the biggest purpose in life. They have so many talents. They are so smart. Kindness comes with ease for them. So the darkness wants to stop them and fight hard to take them away from this earth.

You can be the smartest, brightest person in the room but if you aren't able to feel or understand your feelings, you will not be able to use your talents and skills. Scott was brilliant, maybe one of the most brilliant men I have ever known. He had a huge heart and was kind and good, but his wounds from his past overrode his innate way of being. The daily intake of multiple prescriptions combined with his drinking had stolen his light.

**You don't have to do this alone.**

Find someone who understands you. Lean on those with wisdom and experience. Then ask them how they got out of their darkness. You must ask. You must share and stop suppressing. The suppression is how you lose this battle.

If you are struggling with darkness, if suicidal thoughts are plaguing you, I urge you to seek help. Put an end to suppressing your thoughts and your stress. Share. Reach out. (Click this QR code for access to immediate help). Know that if you lean into support, you can win this battle.

My family and community helped us rise up from the dark times. I forced myself to ask and I got comfortable receiving help. Even once we moved to Arizona we had to find a community. We were lucky to find the best school and a neighborhood that keeps showering us with light and love.

When I lost everything—Scott, my family dream—and had zero in my bank account, that's when God showed up for me. Friends and family sent donations. Many knew that I could not access any of the bank accounts or life insurance and I was not working. These donations gave me hope and I know God had a big role in this. Many were praying for our family and God heard each prayer. You don't have to be affiliated with any religion to pray. I'm talking about sending love and light to someone you wish to send it to. God is my shield and protector. I trust in His path for me and each day ask for His guidance.

We must shine God into others. We must remind them that God is more powerful than darkness.

When you don't ask for help, you open the door to the darkness. You give up and you stop trusting God.

**You must never give up.**

You are not meant to conquer this darkness alone and there is an abundance of healers in the world waiting for you to reach out.

Let me tell you what else worked for me.

God wanted me to know that He will never give up on me. He was listening to my prayers and will listen to yours. He can feel your pain, He can see your fears. He has created you because he believed in you and your purpose in this lifetime. At one time, you also believed in yourself enough to come and accomplish this mission on earth. You were with God and said yes. You knew God would guide you along and that He would never give up on you.

Close your eyes and take three long inhales and exhales and start to remember that God is in you and has never left. There is always a golden thread between you and God. Connect, soften your heart, and shed the armor that you have built around you. This is solely for protection, *not* for isolation. Your mind (ego) needs to trust your heart again. Trust the process and let go of the why. Keep doing this practice until you start to feel again. Allow others near your heart. Your heart will fear this and it will be very uncomfortable at first. It is not ready to get hurt again, but allow love to permeate you from head to toe.

For spiritual growth, you must trust and let go. Then the miracles will start appearing and just one miracle will give you the fire to continue this practice. The flow and ease will be like a dance with God, "A Pas de Deux" (One step for two) like the artist Yongsung Kim painted. Yongsung Kim has said that his work of art will bring you peace, calm, and joy. I love this painting because it reminds me of a vision I had about God and me dancing together through the darkness and out into the light. When I had this vision of me dancing, it made me so happy. I thought it was just because I love to dance, but when I found this painting, I realized what this vision meant.

*A Pas de Deux* by Yongsung Kim. Image courtesy of Havenlight.

Once my faith grew, I let go of my control over things and everything seemed to flow with synchronicity. I was guided and God never gave up on me. His love never left. I just had to remember that I will always be loved. To love myself was to love God.

"Arise, my darling, my beautiful one, and come with me."
—**Song of Songs 2:10**

When you feel you are in a crevice alone and the light is dim, look within and remember you are loved. There is a love out there bigger than you can imagine. Reach for it! Don't give up and don't turn off all the lights. These are the hard lessons and on the other side of the darkness comes joy, peace, and calm.

"Love never gives up on people. It never stops trusting, never loses hope, and never quits."
—**1 Corinthians 13:7**

I saw this with my own family. When pain, anger, and darkness prevailed, love was always the answer. Life would stop and all I concentrated on was pouring love into my kids. School, work, long lists of to-dos were put on hold until my kids would feel loved again. It was all about love. Love from me, friends, teachers, and most of all God healed my children's hearts. To know that they will always be loved was the answer.

**For those of you who love someone who is struggling....**

*Dear friend,*

*I see your heart aching. I see your pure desperation in finding ways to help your loved ones. It is lonely and exhausting. The good days give you so much hope. The bad days are when you have to clean up empty alcohol bottles, garbage on the floor, medication on the counter, or when their anger shows up. You* wonder how you can fix this. It is okay to cry and I see you. If you are isolated and have not connected with friends for a long time, think of who was a dear friend before. Call them. Reconnect. Tell them the truth. You will need community and professional help. You are not alone in this battle and you cannot do this alone. It is too much and too hard when you are isolated. Take care of yourself. Show yourself love. This is not your fault. You cannot fall into their darkness. You must stay strong and heal yourself. You are grieving and you also need to be taken care of.

Love,
Mélissa

# Chapter 27

# Challenge the Resistance

*The lie is that you don't have what it takes to push through the hard.*
*The truth is that God gave you everything you need to fight the resistance.*

**Y**ou are stronger than you think!
**Push through the hard moments!**

God is here to help you progress, not remain stagnant. If life was perfect—no storms, no problems—then progress would never occur.

If you want to build your muscles, it has to be hard. Growth is essential to finding your joy. Push through the shakes when it is your last hold in your workout. You will see the most changes in your body when you push through those last repetitions. It is hard and you have to quiet your inner voice when you want to collapse back on the mat. Then, you have to make sure that you nourish your body properly for that growth to occur as well. The reward for persevering through the hard is happiness and peace. You will be impressed by your accomplishments and you will feel proud of yourself.

At some point, I noticed that things that used to bother me did not anymore. I was able to process conflict and hard work with more ease because I now had the tools to fall back on. I am able to use my knowledge as my best support system. I know these tools worked for me. Not everyone will have the same tool belt but there are definitely similarities.

The problems with our physical health are usually emotional and we must learn how to use the tools that are best for us. Feed your mind and body with rich nutrients that provide light.

# Chapter 28

# Authenticity is the Magnet

> **The lie** is that it is safer to wear a mask.
> **The truth** is that the unveiling of the mask will allow your life to become more fulfilled.

Allow yourself to be truly authentic.
Are you ready to be authentic? It takes courage and dedication to master digging into your soul.

When you are with your closest friend, you can be yourself. Doesn't that feel good? You feel safe and being yourself comes naturally.

Then sometimes you meet with other friends and feel a different energy from them and you start changing the way you react. Or you may not share how you truly feel. You don't feel safe to be yourself. around them You fear they will not like you and will judge you. You move away from your soul and build a barrier. Your light dims. The more you suppress your light, the less alive you feel.

Do you ever notice how some people make you feel? They don't have to talk and you can tell if they are upset with you. Can you feel when someone is not being authentic, not being their true self? I know I can. It is a strong feeling and I tend to want to distance myself.

You can also look within and wonder why you are being affected by that person emotionally. Are they triggering old patterns? Are they hurting your self-esteem? Is your nervous system on high alert while you are with them? It is important to build a barrier for yourself to deflect people that may not have your best interest in mind for you. You have to trust yourself and be confident in who you are. This will create an armor of safety from allowing others to change the way you think about yourself.

Surround yourself only with people who are authentic in their own character. Most of the time these are people who have done the work to heal old wounds. They are confident in who they are and know their purpose.

To become authentic should come easily, but for most it does not. They have many barriers and masks.

Spending time in reflection, meditation, looking within, and growth will allow you to listen to your inner voice. It will shine the light on your purpose and what feels good to you. Everyone has a purpose or a mission in life.

It is important to not sit in fear, anger, guilt, and shame. Release them to allow growth.

Love yourself first and every step toward being authentic will empower you to form true connections and attract the right people.

Choose to act on what feels good to you. Trust yourself.

Let yourself be YOU. Feel the release. Being authentic brings happiness. Speak your truth and you will magnetize those who will lift you up. When you suppress your truth, you will magnetize those who also suppress their truth.

Be who you want to have in your community.

As your community arrives, you will be fortified in their love and authenticity. Loneliness will leave and the support will fill you up.

> "No one can make a fool of you without your consent."
> **—widely attributed to Eleanor Roosevelt**
> *(source unverified)*

# Chapter 29

# The Dreams
# You Stuff Down

*The lie is that dreams never come true.*
*The truth is fear will put a barrier around your dreams.*

The suppression of dreams is just as toxic as the suppression of truth because your dreams ARE a part of your truth. I remember each time I felt a dream rise up inside of me, I couldn't see how it would come true, so I would suppress it. I would push that dream deep within me so that I would never have to hear it again.

There is so much pain in the wanting of a dream that you believe can never happen. That is why we suppress. I know how it feels to wish for a dream to come true and the pain of not seeing or imagining how it could ever happen. I know that dreams can sometimes make you feel crazy, and I know the loneliness that shows up when you have to discard that dream.

While living in Alaska, I dreamt of moving to Arizona where my family and I could enjoy the sun most of the year, we could drive to other states, and my kids could experience a better education. This was my dream: living among palm trees, outdoors most of the year, my kids in a caring learning environment, and my mother living near us. I would look at the homes, schools, hikes, restaurants, and activities available in Arizona. It was fun to dream and research. It brought me joy and excitement.

Dreaming ignites a little flame in your heart and keeps you moving ahead each day. It will feed your soul. Please never stop dreaming and believing that these dreams will come to fruition.

> "Logic will get you from A to B but the imagination will take you everywhere."
> **—Albert Einstein**
> *(widely attributed, source unverified)*

## Chapter 30

# Letting go

> **The lie** is that we must carry all of our traumas with us forever.
> **The truth** is that these traumas may be released and it is possible to live in peace.

The peace that comes from letting go is miraculous. Imagine your life journey is like climbing a mountain and carrying a backpack as you climb a mountain. This backpack holds a rock for each hurt, pain, malicious word that has ever been said to you, or bad thought that you have had about yourself.

By the time you are 20 years old the backpack starts to get heavy.

By 30, the weight is substantial.

By 40, the weight is massive.

Each decade the weight will increase if you don't let go.

You slow down. You are in physical pain from carrying this massive weight.

Anger, fear, anxiety, depression, shame, guilt, doubt, judgment, and revenge will crawl into your mind.

You stop climbing. You are exhausted.

The light of hope gets dimmer and dimmer.

This is YOUR calling to LET GO. Again, ask someone to help you. Pray to God—the creator, your guides, or any name you call that inner source.

Once you reach out, one rock will fall out of your backpack. You will see a sliver of hope.

Once you learn how to release the pain and see that others are also carrying heavy backpacks, you will drop more rocks and see more light.

You will start obtaining more strength to rise back up and continue to climb this mountain. It will be a strenuous hike. You will need to call in more people, books, and knowledge on how to drop more rocks to reach the summit.

An excellent book that will help you to screen your thoughts is *The Myth of Normal* by Gabor Maté, MD.

In screening your thoughts, you will grow and shed your past. Your past will no longer define you. You will not empower those rocks to slow you down anymore.

Soon you will be able to deflect rocks as they come at you. You will build a shield of light around you.

You will be able to continue climbing, feeling peace in your heart. Never stop learning to grow.

I knew in my heart that Scott had to let go, but he would not. He would not let go of the anger, revenge, wanting to be right. I saw the destruction that it created.

That is why when my husband passed, without a doubt, **I LET GO**. One of the best decisions I ever made.

"Practice being **KIND** rather than **RIGHT**."[4] Wayne Dyer said this in one of his speeches. Repeat it until it stays in your thoughts.

Find your soul family, people you want to emulate and who bring out the best in you, people you can be truly authentic with without judgment. Create boundaries for yourself. Never stop seeking growth and knowledge. Find professionals that can help guide you to be the best version of you.

---

[4] Wayne Dyer on *The Quote of the Day Show* with Sean Croxton, episode 1530, "Dr. Wayne Dyer: 'Practice Being Kind Rather Than Right,'"https://seancroxton.com/quote-of-the-day/1490/.

# Chapter 31

# Plant Seeds in Your Kids to Help Them Blossom

*The lie is that children today are incapable.*
*The truth is that children are carbon copies of what they see in front of them.*

Start when your children are at a young age to plant seeds in them—seeds of faith, self-love, community, humility, the ability to give and receive, communication skills, and emotional intelligence. You don't have to teach all of these tools yourself but find a community or mentors that have these similar values. I often wondered how I did not fall into a deep depression. When I travel back to Wasilla, the flood of memories comes back and I am amazed that I was able to maintain a healthy mental state. Now, I realize that it was all those seeds my mother planted in me over the years.

My mother often talked about God, self-love, dreaming big, and never giving up. She often kept us active and playing in nature. We ate healthy home-cooked meals and we never took any pharmaceuticals unnecessarily. My mother's light is bright and you can feel the love that radiates from her. That is her gift: light and love. She instilled in me a positive outlook on life and how we should treat others. This was my foundation and I have carried it throughout my life. This is why I was able to stay in the light.

I am very concerned for our youth these days.

I feel that lack of connection and an overload of commitments create a lonely environment. We have been blessed with wonderful teachers that have poured love into our kids. On the occasions that my kids have had a teacher that they didn't connect with or feel love from, my kids would plummet.

Teachers are already overworked and have large classes, which makes it extremely hard to devote themselves to each of their students. It may be especially hard for a teacher to connect with the students who are struggling the most. Those students keep pushing people away. Nobody understands why these students are behaving this way, but most of the time it is because of a lack of love somewhere in their lives, especially if there was abandonment somewhere in their childhood: grief, divorce, adoption, foster home, neglect from a parent or caretaker.

Depression has been climbing alarmingly high in youth recently and many of them have faced suicide. Kids' mental health is in crisis. Mental Health America studies showed that in 2023, 16.39% of youth aged 12–17 reported suffering from at least one major depressive episode (MDE) in the past year.[5]

---

[5] Mental Health America, Youth Data 2023, https://mhanational.org/issues/2023/mental-health-america-youth-data.

The state prevalence of youth with MDE ranges from 12.57% in New Jersey to 21.13% in Oregon. Now, keep in mind these are just coming from *reported* mental health cases. Can you imagine how many are *not* reported and not seeking help? I remember in Alaska how hard it was to find mental health providers that did not have a long waitlist. Access to different healing modalities were scarce, especially for our youth. When I would speak to other parents, those with teenagers would share that at least one of their children was dealing with depression. It was alarming to me that this had become a pattern in each family. I am heartbroken and confused to hear their stories. Some of these teenagers *are* seeing a counselor now.

My own personal thought is that it is not just one modality that will save them but a collaboration. Surrounding them with faith, love, hope, passion, creativity, and meaning will alleviate the problem.

Most schools do not have a support system for these children who spend eight hours a day there. Many schools do not think it is their responsibility to provide mental health modalities. Schools put the full responsibility on the parents and tell the parents that this is *their* battle to fight. However, we all know that it takes a village to raise kids. Parents cannot do it alone, especially when their child is struggling. Schools are washing their hands clean because this issue is overwhelming and most likely they do not have the finances to incorporate a mental health program.

My dream is to find a solution and to start planting seeds in schools. What if we start in elementary and high school classes to teach mental health healing modalities. Teach them nervous system reset tools and stress resiliency. Help them with self-love and affirmations. Coach them to watch their thoughts. Get them to connect with fellow students and create pods with those they connect with the most. Help them to be creative in art, dance, music, and writing. Help them find their passion in life, and find meaning so they can feel loved and connected. A group of trained individuals could come in and teach these students and teachers. We could provide seminars for teachers to teach them these tools too, so that they can incorporate them into class for their students and themselves. Teachers are overworked, underpaid, and need support too. They can lose their passion when they are not shown love for their work. They are helping us raise our next generation, so why is it so hard to provide them with more funding and increase their salary?

# A Final Message
# from a Friend

I want to extend my heartfelt gratitude to you, reader, for taking the time to read my book. Writing this book was a big part of my healing process and I now recommend to everyone to write daily. Even just a quick note on your phone would provide a way to release emotions. Only one thought a day of gratitude can help shift your mood; write it down or say it out loud. You could even write your own book just for yourself and your growth process. I think the hardest part of writing this book was the editing and finally deciding that I am ready to publish it. Releasing this book to the world brings a level of vulnerability that has been extremely hard to overcome. I've combated intense fear, overthinking, and being scared of others' judgments or opinions. I had to keep focused on my why—my purpose—and keep praying. This allowed me to trust and let go of the fear, anxiety, and avoidance of the edits and review.

I chose not to be a prisoner of my fears. Fears could have paralyzed me from achieving growth or reaching my best life!

I was already aware that fear could weaken my immune system, cause cardiovascular damage or gastrointestinal problems. I had gone through these before, experiencing: gut issues, vulnerability to viruses, sharp pain in my heart, palpitations, hair loss, premature graying in my hair. I will not let fear take over my life anymore. I surrender to God's calling.

I trust in God's promise to strengthen me and will continue to pray daily.

I will always be evolving and I know this is only the beginning of my story. I am an open book now because there is immense power in sharing my story. I have made many mistakes along my journey but I am not letting them cripple me and preventing me from climbing higher. They will not hold me back from my purpose in life. I will always be mindful of my EGO; as Wayne Dyer said, "EGO means Edging God Out."[6]

My hope is that I encourage you to dig deeper into who you are and to live your truth. To shift your perspective daily and to be mindful of your thoughts. Rewiring your thoughts takes a daily commitment and practice. My belief is that God has planted a seed in everyone and we must look within us to allow that seed to flourish. Once we see our purpose clearly, that vision will give us the courage and strength to face the challenges along the road. It will keep us on the right path toward the road of happiness. If you are not following your purpose, life will try to redirect you along the way until you listen to your soul. Manifest acceptance, and surrender to God's lead. Grab onto His hand and follow in His footsteps.

---

[6] Wayne Dyer on *The Quote of the Day Show* with Sean Croxton, episode 1530, "Dr. Wayne Dyer: 'Practice Being Kind Rather Than Right,'"https://seancroxton.com/quote-of-the-day/1490/.

With this faith in God as your foundation, you will find yourself surviving through the storms.

*I am sending you off with gratitude. Love yourself deeply and seek your truth. Don't hesitate to reach out to me. I am ready to be the source for you to share your story. I am not a professional but a resource and would be honored to be yours.*

*With love and light,*

*Mélissa*

"Life is a series of tests which, if squarely faced, give us greater mental strength and peace of mind. Learn to rely more on your Heavenly Father for guidance and understanding. Fill your empty moments with love for Him, and you will *know* that you are not alone."[7]
—**Paramahansa Yogananda**

---

[7] Paramahansa Yogananda, "Paramahansa Yogananda, Chapters 1–5," *Royal Science of God-Realization: The immortal dialogue between soul and Spirit, A New Translation and Commentary*, (Los Angeles: Self-Realization Fellowship, 1999 Second Edition), 253.

A CELEBRATION OF
*Life*

Scott Allen Methven

August 8th, 1974 - March 13, 2022.

Best Boss!

#nationalbossday